101 WAYS TO
BETTER
COMMUNICATION

ELIZABETH TIERNEY

**KOGAN
PAGE**

<u>YOURS TO HAVE AND TO HOLD</u>
BUT NOT TO COPY

First published in 1998

Apart from any fair dealing for the purposes of research or private study, or criticism or review, as permitted under the Copyright, Designs and Patents Act 1988, this publication may only be reproduced, stored or transmitted, in any form or by any means, with the prior permission in writing of the publishers, or in the case of reprographic reproduction, in accordance with the terms and licences issued by the Copyright Licensing Agency. Enquiries concerning reproduction outside those terms should be sent to the publishers at the undermentioned address:

Kogan Page Limited
120 Pentonville Road
London N1 9JN

© Elizabeth Tierney 1998

The right of Elizabeth Tierney to be identified as the author of this work has been asserted by her in accordance with the Copyright, Designs and Patents Act 1988.

British Library Cataloguing in Publication Data

A CIP record for this book is available from the British Library.

ISBN 0 7494 2404 4

Typeset by Kogan Page
Printed and bound in Great Britain by Clays Ltd, St Ives plc

Contents

Introduction

Right now, all over the world, people are doing business. While you read this page, hundreds, indeed thousands of business meetings are in progress. Busy people are sending faxes, typing e-mails, opening letters, reading reports, drafting memos, talking with colleagues, addressing conferences, or chatting over coffee or tea. They are communicating, and communication is the life blood of organizations. Even though we communicate all the time, most of us have not been trained to do so. Each of us can improve.

This book offers *101 Ways to Better Communication*. It is written for business people who recognize how vital effective communication is to their own success and to the success of their organizations. While each of the 101 ways considers a different aspect of communication, you will benefit most if you view them all as a whole.

While you are reading through this book, other business people may be discussing missions, goals, losses, profits, overheads, policies, budgets, loans, promotions, strategic plans, product development, training, hiring, technology, downsizing, take-overs, global competitiveness, office parties, desk arrangements, coffee breaks, or office supplies. Imagine what the implications are if you can't understand what is being discussed in board rooms, in offices, at lunch tables. Imagine the implications if your colleagues don't understand your views or can't articulate their own. Whether you are ordering paper for the copier or making long-range hiring plans, if communication fails, the outcome is confusion. Therefore, let's examine ways of ensuring a happier outcome.

Part One: Communication in General

While the second section of this book examines specific types of communication, this section is devoted to improving your understanding of communication in general. It suggests different ways of gaining insights into communication by examining principles, theories, organization, language, attitudes and behaviour

Most of us take the process of communicating for granted. For good reason. After all, we have been doing it throughout our lives: at home, in a shop, on the bus, in the airport, in the office or at school. Although we communicate all the time, we don't always communicate successfully. We know this to be true because of the frequency with which we hear or use phrases like:

> 'What did you mean by... ?'
> 'But I thought you said... '
> 'Could you clarify that last point?'
> 'At the meeting didn't you indicate that you... ?'
> 'But I assumed that you were suggesting... '
> 'I'm sorry, I misunderstood.'

Each of these phrases suggests mis-communication, an undesirable situation in any office. So what can you do to minimize this problem?

One
Benefits of Better Communication

Let's begin our discussion by considering how you could benefit from better communication. Before we do that, let's clarify two words that are used throughout the book: 'audience' and 'message'. Audience refers to the people with whom you are communicating – one, one thousand or more. Message refers to the notion that you want to share with your audience. One message might be 'Good morning,' another might be your annual report to shareholders. With message and audience in mind, let us begin.

WAY 1   SAVE RESOURCES

Poor communication wastes time and money and affects morale and productivity. Effective communication, on the other hand, saves time and money and has a positive impact on people. Consider the following scenario:

On Wednesday Frank promises Loraine that he will have Gary send her a copy of a confidential report. It includes data for her presentation on Friday. However, Frank forgets to tell Gary to give the report to her.

What happens?

When Loraine doesn't receive the report, she calls Frank or Gary to ask for it. If she phones Frank first, he may say that he is sorry, that he'll send it along promptly. If she phones Gary first, he may not have a clue as to what she is talking about. In the meantime Loraine's work is delayed; she's counting on the data in the report. Gary is bewildered. Not having spoken to Frank, Gary isn't sure whether her request for a confidential document is legitimate. So now what? Phone calls or e-mail ensue: from Gary to Frank, from Gary to Loraine, from Frank to Loraine. Priorities change. Work is stopped or interrupted – all because of a minor failure to communicate. Gary is annoyed and embarrassed. Loraine is frustrated, under pressure and angry. Frank feels guilty.

Scenarios like these happen in business all the time. We are human and make mistakes. Imagine if each one of us failed to communicate accurately with only one of our many colleagues just once a day. Multiply those slip-ups by thousands of interactions. The implications of all those slip-ups or disruptions could be staggering. As a result, what invariably occurs is that what we planned to do when we came to work in the morning is postponed. Instead we are seeking clarification of someone's message, report, notice, document, or phone call.

Let's alter the original scenario. Frank did tell Gary to send Loraine the report and Gary, in fact, sent it. However, after forwarding the report, Gary noticed an error on a table on page 12 – a transposition of some numbers. Now what? We have more phone calls and more frustration. We have apologizing, correcting, photocopying, collecting incorrect reports, writing covering notes, distributing revisions, and phoning to explain the error – all time-consuming.

Think about your own experiences:

- Ever had to read a memo twice because you couldn't make sense of it after the first reading?
- Ever had to read a memo out loud in an effort to understand it?
- Ever had to phone colleagues to see if they understood what was said at a meeting?
- Ever received a follow-up memo written to clarify an earlier one?
- Ever had to attend an impromptu meeting called to explain the information that was distributed in a memo?

If you answered 'yes' to any of these, then you know that mis-communication is wasteful. Better communication might have avoided the problems. Rather than spending time clarifying, apologizing, chasing missing reports, photocopying, shredding paper or making unnecessary phone calls, you can focus on what you had planned to do when you arrived at work. Mis-communication makes people feel unsure, angry, confused, embarrassed, disgusted, frustrated or humiliated. That's the human cost. More careful communication uses your resources more effectively.

WAY 2   BE CLEAR

Business involves influencing others. To be successful requires clarity. For instance:

- when you counsel an employee about lateness, you are encouraging that person to change;
- when you make a presentation to prospective clients, you are convincing them that your recommendations meet their needs;
- when you write a progress report, you are informing others about what transpired over a period of time and clarifying why specific actions were appropriate.

Annual reports, inter-office memos, faxes, e-mail, chats, staff meetings are all opportunities to persuade. Therefore, we should clarify matters.

The more precise you are, the more accurate your communication. Your audience will better understand what you intended and will be better able to act on your message. They will also feel more secure knowing that what they are doing is what you expect them to do.

Ever read a notice that created confusion because it didn't include the date, place and time of the meeting? If the message had been accurate, operations would have been smoother. You would have known what was expected.

Clarity enables you to do your job without excessive questioning, anxiety or second-guessing. Rather than having to restate your ideas three or four times to make your point, better communication enables you to express your ideas clearly the first time.

WAY 3   BE CREDIBLE AND PROFESSIONAL

Good communicators save resources, enable others to understand their responsibilities, and are credible and professional. Have you ever had supervisors ask you to work on projects and not given you any ideas about what was expected? The fact is when you know the purpose and the parameters of an assignment, you know where to begin. It is also easier to work with someone who is straightforward and organized. As we said, it is less stressful to know the time, date, place, and agenda of the next meeting rather than being called to impromptu ones all the time.

We are grateful to managers who are thoughtful communicators, who plan and think through issues; they, are respected for their sensitivity to the commitment of others. Think about your colleagues. Which of them do you consider to be the most professional? How does their communication style affect your opinion? Those people we admire are usually good listeners, thoughtful, polished, organized, clear and to the point.

As professionals we don't like wasting time. We make decisions around time. For example, when we have several reports to read, we usually start with those that are written clearly and succinctly. Why? Because such reports require only one reading, while poorly written documents may require two or three.

We welcome meetings that are well run and well organized. We dread others. It's not the issues that make us balk; it's the endless tangential discussions.

We appreciate those people who get to the point promptly compared to those others who ramble on for 35 minutes – or longer. When we return phone calls, it isn't always our knowledge of priorities that governs our decisions about which ones to return first. We phone, in part, based on our experience of past phone calls.

We make judgements about who is credible and professional. We want others to respect us as well.

WAY 4   USE COMMUNICATION CHANNELS WELL

We can communicate in many ways. But in a given situation one way may be better than another. Sometimes it is better to talk than to write:

- a telephone call may be more prudent on some occasions than a fax;
- a chat may be more efficient than a phone call;
- a memo may be more practical than a meeting;
- a face-to-face meeting may have more impact than a letter or an e-mail message;

- a hand-written note may be more effective than a type-written one because it may seem more personal;
- having someone else run a meeting or prepare an agenda may empower others to take charge.

Good communicators are sensitive to the nuances of diverse communication channels. They make educated decisions about what is most appropriate for a situation given the individuals involved. What determines the choice? Distance, urgency, confidentiality, relationships, politics, complexity or cost may affect your decision. Considering channels of communication:

- Would you send a memo to staff announcing a fire in the photocopying room?
- Would you e-mail a subordinate to tell him that he is being made redundant?
- Would you call a meeting of department heads to announce that the staff dining room is going to be repainted over the weekend?
- Would you send a letter to an overseas distributor indicating that there is a dangerous flaw in the product?

Ineffective communicators do not always recognize all the options available. Sometimes they use inappropriate ones. They always write or they always phone. They put information into the grapevine rather than make a formal announcement. They wait rather than hurry. They create records where there should be none. They ask assistants to do what they as managers should do. Such decisions affect the organization. Better communicators use communication channels well.

Two
Basic Principles

Underlying effective communications are three principles. First, you should recognize the importance of valuing relationships you have or want in business. Second, you should realize that you will have to make many decisions about your communication. Third, you should accept the notion of the importance of practicing your skills. Let's examine the three basic principles.

WAY 5   VALUE RELATIONSHIPS

Business involves establishing and maintaining relationships. Effective communicators weigh the relationships that they have with their audience. You establish relationships for the short term or maintain them over the long term. You may want to rid yourself of a problematic relationship, such as the bully in your department who cannot take direction. Whenever you communicate, think about the relationship that you have with your audience. Ask yourself what you are trying to accomplish. Are you trying to win over a new client? Influence an old client? Train a new employee? Advise a senior partner? Assuage a disgruntled customer?

How you communicate with these people affects these relationships. And you know there are consequences to treating people well or treating them thoughtlessly. How would you feel if:

- You had been made to wait for 20 minutes even though you had arrived on time for a meeting?
- If you had to speak to someone who is chewing gum on the phone or who made you feel as if you were interrupting a private conversation?
- If you made a suggestion at a meeting and no one reacted to your ideas?
- If you have a colleague who always hangs up the phone

without a 'good-bye'?
- If you were made to stand when everyone else in the room is seated?

How you communicate can make people feel important or unimportant. You can make people feel good or bad. You can make people feel demeaned or respected. And don't forget that people share their experiences. Unhappy customers share their unhappiness with other customers. Frustrated clients tell other clients about their anger or disappointment. Rejected candidates associate their experiences with your products or services. Disaffected employees complain to each other. Disgusted purchasers won't come back at all.

Therefore, whether it is a phone call, writing a letter or memo, or engaging in conversation, think about how your communication style affects the relationships that you currently have and those that you want to have. Whether you are reporting to your boss, addressing the board, speaking to a secretary or handyman, consider the consequences of your style.

Recall interactions you have had with clients or colleagues. Consider how their communication styles affected your working relationships.

WAY 6   MAKE DECISIONS

Before you communicate, take the time to make informed decisions. Too often we act first and think later. Get in the habit of asking yourself some basic questions. The questions are the tried and true: who, what, why, when and how.

Who? Ask yourself with whom are you communicating. Be aware of the demographics of your audience. Having that data helps you determine the best way to communicate your message. When it is pertinent find out the age, sex, education, nationality, job title, the relationship of the audience to you and to any others present. Knowing about your audience helps you decide on your words, approaches or analogies. Will you be insulting intelligence by explaining too much? Will you be speaking over their heads? Will you be using language that they don't know? Or will you be discussing issues with which they are familiar?

What? Ask yourself what information you want to share. Then, decide how much information is sufficient to make the point you want to make. Determine what background to the material or details have to be to communicated to ensure the audience's understanding.

Why? Ask yourself why you are sharing what you are saying, drawing or writing. Decide on your motivation. Has an incident prompted a change of plan or policy? Are you anticipating concerns because additional staff are being hired? Have there been staff problems adjusting to a new approach to supervision? Are you encouraging or rewarding entrepreneurial thinking? Are you counselling someone who has been away ill?

When? Ask yourself what is the time of day, the day of the week or the time of the year. Decide how the timing might affect your message. Are people under pressure because it is the end of a quarter? Is it just before a holiday or AGM? People react differently at different times.

How? Ask yourself how you should share what you want to communicate. Decide which method is best for the given situation and the individuals involved. Is speed important? Is face-to-face or voice-to-voice contact essential? Is thorough documentation demanded? Is distance a factor? Is conversation over coffee the best approach or would a formal meeting be better?

Effective communicators reflect on the situation and make appropriate decisions before they communicate.

WAY 7   PRACTISE YOUR SKILLS

Athletes and musicians practise. Business people should too. Practice develops your communication skills.

- If you write e-mails frequently, learn what is and what is not effective on the computer.
- Are short notes better than long ones?
- Is upper and lower case easier to read than all capitals?
- If you find yourself frequently giving talks and presentations, develop your speaking talents.
- If you write reports and memos, concentrate on your writing skills.
- If you appraise, interview or counsel, focus on improving your listening and questioning techniques.

Because few of us are taught to write technical reports or to make business presentations, consider taking courses and reading books. Become self-aware. As you get to know yourself better, work on diminishing your weaknesses and enhancing your skills.

Three
Communicating – the Theory

By examining the theory behind the communication process, you can objectively examine your daily interactions. Doing so is one of the best ways of improving your communication abilities. The theory describes how communication works in abstract terms. It describes what actually transpires when we communicate. The process begins with your having a message that you want to transmit to your audience. That audience receives it, reacts to it and eventually gives you feedback. That response may then lead to another message, another and so on.

WAY 8   HAVE A MESSAGE

What is a message? As we know by now, it is a thought, an idea, a feeling. The first step is to have a message you want to share with someone else.

- A message can be as simple – it can say 'hello' or 'I love you'.
- A message can be straightforward – a warning to 'mind the gap' on the underground.
- A message can be complex – a series of recommendations for restructuring your business.
- A message can be brief – it can be a few words in an e-mail.
- A message can be lengthy – a 250 page report, a 30 minute speech.

What you want to share with one, several or multitudes of individuals is the message.

WAY 9   MAKE CHOICES

Suppose you have a message you want to share. Now make choices. Decide how best to convey your ideas. The next step in the communication process involves your deciding whether you should use words, symbols, gestures or images. You, the sender, decide how best to convey it. Suppose you want to say, 'I love you.' You have to decide if you want to give the person a hug, say the words out loud, or write them on a Valentine card.

We send messages all the time to colleagues in our offices, across town or across the ocean. Whether you are sending them over the radio or via satellite into a living room, you make choices about whether words, gestures, symbols or images would be best. You decide whether written words, spoken words or photographic images would make the point. But then, maybe gestures would be better. Your choices need to fit the situations.

- Would you draw pictures, use spoken language or hand gestures to assist a 767 land on the tarmac?
- Would you use words, images or gestures to conduct an orchestra and make the musicians change tempo?
- Would you use words, images or gestures to praise or reprimand a subordinate?
- Would you use words, images or gestures to convince a new client of the effectiveness of your organization?

You the communicator decide which medium to use. Should the conductor send an e-mail? Would you expect the pilot to read a memo? By thinking about your audience, you determine which words to use, which images to select or which gestures to make. You choose.

WAY 10   SEND YOUR MESSAGE

You know what you want to communicate. Now, how should you send it? You have many options about how to get your message to your audience:

- you can give a speech to a group;
- you can dash off a memo via the internet;
- you can distribute a 50 page report through inter-office mail;
- you can write a fax and send it;
- you can make a phone call;
- you can write a letter and post it;
- you can wave across the corridor;

- you can wink to a colleague after a meeting;
- you can call a formal meeting in your office;
- you can chat in the hall.

Each of these represents a way of sending a message to your audience. You make the choice about what is the most effective method of sending it.

WAY 11   EXPECT FEEDBACK

Up to now, you have been in charge of the process. You have been making all the decisions and weighing the choices. Once the message leaves your lips or is put in an inter-office envelope, your control of the process is over for the moment. It shifts to the audience. Your message is in their hands or minds. They, not you, will interpret and react to your message. And react they will. Their reactions to your message is your feedback.

- If you tell a joke, your audience may or may not laugh.
- If you provide written recommendations to your clients, they may accept or reject them.
- If you propose a new policy to the board, they may or may not approve.
- If you make a sales pitch, consumers may or may not buy.
- If you draw a picture, the audience may misunderstand or misinterpret it.

You, the sender, cannot control what your audience, the receiver of your message, does. As you can see, the audience gives you feedback in different ways:

- no one laughs when you tell a joke;
- the board wants to have further discussion;
- the client is enthusiastic about your recommendations.

Listen, look for and weigh what those reactions meant. Perhaps the audience didn't understand your meaning. Maybe your frame of reference wasn't clear. In addition, notice what questions you were asked. Were they on one specific aspect or on several areas of what you said or wrote? Did people seem confused by your message? Did you receive a memo asking for clarification? Did you get no reaction whatsoever? Were your letters, e-mails or faxes unanswered? Whatever the responses you get, recognize them as feedback. Learn from them. They are telling you that an aspect of your message was clear or it was not. Perhaps your report was too long, too short, too vague, too detailed or just right. Your talk was on target or tangential. Your counselling session was misunderstood. Whatever your message, expect feedback.

WAY 12   THINK ABOUT THE AUDIENCE

Focus on the audience. Too often, we as communicators are self-absorbed. We are more concerned with how we look and sound than with how the audience is reacting to our message. Focus on the audience and articulate your message as accurately as possible with that unique group or individual in mind.

You would not knowingly speak Japanese to an audience that understands no Japanese, display paintings to the sightless, or play music to the deaf. In the same way you should not forget that some jargon, certain technical vocabulary, specific images, gestures and words may not be understood or interpreted in the same way by everyone. Keep your audience in mind.

WAY 13   ANTICIPATE AUDIENCE REACTION

Effective communicators are sensitive to reaction, are aware of differing interpretations of what they wish to communicate and anticipate the audience's reaction. Once you have determined your message and the mode of transmission, put yourself in the audience's place. Ask yourself: will they accept what I want to communicate? Just as effective salespeople listen for and anticipate objections, you should too.

Prepare for possible arguments you will encounter. Are you presenting complex ideas? Will any part of the message confuse or overwhelm?

Look for numbers or percentages that may bewilder the audience.

See if a concept is fraught with too many technical implications for people to absorb.

Anticipate emotional responses. Some people may be worried, delighted or angered by your ideas. Will shareholders attend a meeting already angry because of the past performance of the company? Will they attend delighted by past performance and expect to hear more good news and thus, be unable or unwilling to hear negative information that may affect profits? Anticipate that your messages may require significant background information. Some people may be worried, delighted or angered by your ideas.

Before uttering it, consider how your message will be received by the audience for whom it is intended. Will you worry the audience? Will you delight them? Will some people become nervous, while others relax? The more you can anticipate reaction, the less likely that your ideas will be met with bewilderment or anger.

Four
Blocking Communication

You want to be sure that your message is received by others exactly as you sent it. You want it to arrive intact, and you want it to be understood. Thinking about some of the ways that communication can be blocked enables you to prevent the blockage. Let's look at five ways that interfere with effective communication.

WAY 14   BE UNCLEAR

The easiest way to block communication is to waffle. Can you recall politicians or instructors you couldn't understand because they used endless high-blown terms or indecipherable abstractions? Have you ever read books or listened to speeches that fit those categories? At the time we probably wondered what was wrong with us rather than with the person attempting to communicate. Most likely the problem wasn't with you, but rather with the speakers, instructors or writers. They were not taking their audience into consideration when they conveyed their messages. They were making incorrect assumptions about what we understand. Many messages are loaded with abstractions that give us no opportunity to grasp the concepts in simple terms.Corporate mission statements provide us with prime illustrations of unclear language. Such statements are about vision, trust and responsibility. Unfortunately, many are written in such high-blown language and convoluted sentence structures they end up having little or no meaning for the people involved in the day-to-day operation of an organization, one of the constituencies for which the statement is designed.

Imagine a situation in which Martin meets with his boss for 45 minutes. The agenda is to discuss Martin's future. At the end of the meeting Martin still doesn't know if his contract is being renewed. Two weeks later Martin is still wondering and waiting for his new contract. What could have happened at the meeting? Did Martin not hear what was said? Did the boss not articulate the message clearly enough?

Think about the number of ways we can confuse, cause anxiety or foster second-guessing simply by being unclear.

WAY 15 MAKE POOR CHOICES

Another way of confusing or losing your audience is to select vague or inappropriate words or images for a given situation. Consider:

> 'It would appear that we have some concerns with regard to the budget.'
> 'We need to consider the implications of what transpired.'
> 'It is important that we follow through on those kinds of issues.'

In each instance the audience has only vague notions of what was intended by the speaker. What are the 'concerns' in the budget? What aspect of the budget is causing the concern? What are the 'implications'? What has 'transpired'? What 'kinds of issues'? What kind of 'follow through' is important?

Too often communicators make assumptions about what other people understand. Consider the little phrases: 'Is it half ten or is it 10:30'? Do you want a coffee to 'take out' or 'take away'? In a shop are you 'all right' or 'do you need any help'? Choosing phrases as simple as these may create confusion.

Rather than grasping your ideas immediately, the audience will spend time interpreting your meaning. If you were to show them a blurred photograph, give them a graph with no title, or misuse language, they will waste time. In such circumstances your audience cannot understand what you intended. You might just as well be speaking a foreign language to those who don't know a word of it. You have made poor choices.

WAY 16 SELECT THE WRONG MEDIUM

Another way to ensure that your message is blocked is to select the wrong communication medium. As we noted earlier:

- airport ground crews don't send faxes to a pilot taxiing a plane down the runway;
- you do not want your secretary to type all your urgent phone messages and then give them to you at the end of the week;
- you wouldn't call a meeting to be held at the end of January to express condolences to a colleague who had lost a loved one in December.

Given the numerous choices available to us, it is easy to make unwise decisions about how we are going to communicate a particular message. Perhaps we took too long to answer, were too impersonal in our response, created a record when omitting to do so would have been wiser, or failed to document when we should have. As a consequence, we may have sent the wrong message entirely.

We may have appeared thoughtless or callous or finding ourselves wishing that we could shred documents. Communication was blocked because we chose the wrong medium.

WAY 17   LOSE THE MESSAGE

Another way to block communication is to lose the message – literally to lose it. This can happen in many ways:

- you may not hear someone who speaks too softly;
- a letter posted to the wrong address may be lost;
- faxes can be blurred or have missing pages;
- e-mail may be undeliverable because the address you have been given is unknown or not in a directory;
- telephone messages may not be recorded on the answering machine, deleted too quickly from the voice mail or lost in a pile of papers on a desk;
- reports may be distributed to the wrong offices;
- construction noise in the room next door may prevent you from hearing what was said in your own office.

In essence, communication can be blocked because the message did not reach the other party.

WAY 18   ALIENATE THE AUDIENCE

Another way to block communication is to offend your audience. It is easy to do – deliberately or inadvertently. If the audience takes offence at some part of your message, you risk their not listening to the rest of it. Worse, they may not listen to future messages.

You can alienate an audience by patronizing them, by treating them as if they weren't intelligent enough to understand you.

You can demean them by what you say or what you do. Suppose you say, 'Well, you have worked here only a year, so you couldn't possibly understand!', 'You mean you don't follow rugby. Really!' or 'The solution is obvious', or 'You marketing people don't understand the bottom line.'

- You can offend your audience by not looking at them when you speak to them. You can put people off by sitting while they stand, or by forgetting names.
- You can alienate them by not sharing information, by not telling them the truth or by not paying attention to what they are saying.
- You can also put them off with your body language. The speaker who lifts his chin, puts his nose in the air and then intones great truths to an unseen audience puts people off.
- Your clothing can offend, too. Ever wondered how important you are to visitors when they arrive in your office poorly groomed?
- You can put people off by telling an inside joke or anecdote. While four of the five people may know what you are talking about, the fifth person is at a loss and may feel bewildered by the others' reaction.
- You can put people off when you fumble in your pocket and then produce dog-eared or scribbled notes. Your audience will wonder how much time and effort was taken to prepare. Did you do your work in the taxi on the way over?

Audiences notice such things and are turned off. Even if your ideas are well intentioned, if your audience is offended in some way, they may not listen to you.

Five
Unblocking Communication

As we have noted, it is easy to block communication. Therefore, if your goal is for your audience to think about your message and respond to it, then minimize the chances for failed communication. Let's look at six ways of unblocking communication.

WAY 19   PREPARE

Unclear messages can block communication. To prevent that you have to take time to be accurate. You have to prepare. Suppose you want to discuss the issue of lateness with some members of your staff. Before you rapidly begin to draft memos or call meetings about lateness, you should take the time to determine precisely what aspect of lateness you want to address.

- Do you want to discuss the impact of tardiness on other workers in specific departments?
- Do you want to recommend a new policy because lateness is affecting the morale of people who are coming in on time?
- Do you want to implement a policy to progressively discipline those individuals who are coming in late?

It is not enough to have a general idea about the subject. Refine your thoughts, so that you have a precise topic. That way you can be specific and provide appropriate data to support your thoughts rather than rambling on, talking about generalities as many people do. Refining your thoughts is part of preparation.

WAY 20   KNOW YOUR PURPOSE

To be sure your communication is not blocked, think through what you are trying to accomplish with your note, fax, memo, report, e-mail or phone call. Remember that you are trying to communicate a message to produce a desired response.

- Perhaps your message is intended to motivate the staff, so as to complete a task as quickly as possible.
- Perhaps you want to prevent divisiveness.
- Perhaps you are encouraging teamwork.
- Perhaps you are justifying your recommendation, explaining a procedure or policy that has caused confusion.
- Are you creating competition between teams or divisions?
- Are you empathizing?
- Are you clarifying a situation?
- Are you rectifying an error?

Know your purpose – effective communicators do.

Let's spend a minute with Margaret. Suppose she decides to say 'Good Morning' to the president of the company who happens to be walking by her in the corridor. Her motivation may be varied:

- Margaret thinks that it is polite to greet people she passes, or
- she wants to be noticed, or
- she was recently counselled about appearing unfriendly to others, or
- she is feeling good about the day and wants to share her feelings, or
- she is following company policy to greet all colleagues.

In any event Margaret has sent her 'good morning' message, to the president. She alone knows why she did. In the same way you should know exactly why you are sending memos and e-mails. You should know the purpose of your reports, your talks, your conversations. Good communicators do.

Assume that you do decide to meet with your department in order to discuss lateness. Ask yourself exactly what aspect of lateness you are addressing. Then ask yourself why you are addressing the issue. If you don't know, if you can't articulate your purpose, then don't be surprised when people leave your meeting asking each other, 'What was that meeting all about?' Rather than resolving the lateness problem, your audience will be spending time second guessing your intentions. Be clear in your own mind about what you hope to accomplish. Know your purpose.

WAY 21 ANALYSE YOUR AUDIENCE

We cannot say it enough: know your audience. Learn as much about them as you can. Do your own demographic study. If you are facing a small group, find out who they are.

- What are their names?
- Ask if a report you are writing is being sent to native English speakers or to individuals for whom English is a second language.
- Is your audience male? Female? Mixed?
- What are their ages?
- What is the education level of the people?
- What do they know about you, your organization and your subject?

Obtaining this information helps you tailor your thoughts specifically to them. You can make explanations that will be relevant to them.

Be relevant. If you want to explain the negotiations process to a group of children, don't use the example of purchasing a house. Provide an example, but choose a meaningful one for the audience. The average 10-year-old is not a home buyer. Negotiating to stay up late and watch television might be more relevant. The more relevant you can be, the more likely it is that the audience will grasp your concepts.

Understand the relationship of the members of the audience to you and to each other in addition to understanding a group's demography. Ask yourself about the politics of the situation.

- Who is going to be reading what you have written?
- Who else might be given a copy? Why?
- Who will influence what you are trying to accomplish? How will that happen?

Consider the organizational dynamics.

- Who is looking for a promotion and may want to speak out and shine? How can that person be useful to you?
- Who resents you and may take pot-shots at your ideas?
- Who is jealous or threatened?

- Who has nothing to lose?
- Who is tired or under stress?
- Whose ideas are more respected than others?
- Who rarely says anything but is always on target when he or she does?
- Which people speak because they enjoy the sound of their own voices?
- Who has been asked to stand in for someone else?
- Who has authority? Who doesn't?

Understand the organizational structure and know how it affects your audience. Be sensitive to the unspoken patterns of influence and the role that personality plays in group interaction. The more you know about your audience, the more effective you can be.

WAY 22 MAKE GOOD CHOICES

Learn what you can about the person on the other end of the phone or in front of the computer terminal on the other side of the ocean. Then make the best choices you can. You decide to use words in your message rather than images. You decide whether to use English, French, German or Chinese. Having done so, select words which will be best understood by the other parties. If you are talking about computer technologies to individuals who are not computer literate, you cannot assume that they know the language. Take the time to explain terms. However, if you are talking to people who have been intimately involved with computer development over the last 20 years, explanations may not be necessary.

In the same way, if you discuss issues that date back five years and your audience consists of people who are new to the organization, then provide historical background. If, on the other hand, they are senior people, a brief review might be more than adequate. In addition, if you use terms that are idiomatic to your culture, non-natives may not understand. While you can say that you are putting an issue on the long finger in Ireland, you have to put it on the back burner in the US. If you believe that everyone present understands American football, it would be appropriate for you to use analogies from that sport. However, if they aren't familiar with that game and rugby is their game of choice, then describing business strategy in terms of American football may be lost on your audience.

The more you think about your audience, the better your choices should be. The better your choices, the greater the chances that your message will be understood.

WAY 23   SEND YOUR MESSAGE WISELY

By now you know what you want to say and why you want to say it. You also know more about your audience. Given that information, decide on the best way to communicate. Focus once again on your audience. Think about the numbers, personalities, issues, politics, knowledge, relationships, diversity, immediacy, confidentiality and distance. Given all those variables, consider how best to transmit your message.

Decide if your message is essential for everyone you work with or just for some. Should your ideas be sent in a memo distributed to heads of departments? Or would a meeting of the heads of departments be better?

Decide if you want to create an opportunity for open discussion. Consider if it is important that people hear your voice or see your face. Do you want to make a video tape in order to present your ideas? Would it be better to phone? Do you want to invite or avoid questions? Perhaps e-mailing everyone in the organization would be an efficient way. Based on the nature of your message and on the composition of your audience, make an informed decision about how you will send your message.

WAY 24   IDENTIFY BARRIERS

You are aware of potential blockages to communication, so anticipate as many of them as you can. Consider what might interfere with your efforts to get your message across. Will you encounter contextual issues or people problems?

Know yourself. Are there aspects of your personal style that create problems? Do you have a booming voice? Do you whisper?

Know your office. Do you share one and so have little privacy? Are your responses delayed because your phone lines are so busy? Is your assistant polite?

Know your equipment. Are reports delayed because of the endless queue at the photocopier? Is your copying equipment slow? Can the word processor handle the volume of material that your office produces?

Know the organization. Are there political problems? Have some of your colleagues been bypassed for promotion and are bitter or angry? Is there a current union dispute which is distracting people?

Know the calendar. Is it Friday before a long holiday weekend? Is it Monday following a holiday break?

Know people. Are you communicating with a new client, an angry client, a frustrated client? Are you communicating with people who are tired, resentful or looking for advancement? Have you little time to communicate your message? Identify those aspects of work that create barriers. Then, do the best you can to overcome them.

Six
Organizing your Thoughts

It will be easier for your audience to understand you if you have had time to prepare your thoughts. The more organized you are, the more thoughtful your message will be and the more likely it is that your audience will grasp your ideas. Let's consider seven ways that should make your communication more focused.

WAY 25   ESTABLISH THE CONTEXT

Bring your audience into the picture by establishing the context of your ideas. Early in your communication, provide your audience with enough information to allow them to understand what is about to follow. Remember they are thinking of other issues: calls to return, memos to write, budgets to finish or videos to return.

Think about the opening scenes of films and TV shows. Many film makers bring you into the story quickly using a number of methods. For example, you may first see a city from the air. Then the camera focuses on landmarks: the Eiffel Tower, Mount Fuji, the Houses of Parliament, or the Washington Monument. You know where you are. Then the camera moves into the streets, into a particular building or into a car. Once inside, you meet the characters and are rapidly brought into the story. Other films provide a title for an opening shot indicating the location and the time. Both techniques bring the audience into the picture. Do the same thing. Whether you use a memo, fax, e-mail, a report or talk, establish the context. When you do, you help the audience focus on your message. Establishing the context provides the audience with enough information to understand how your message connects to what they already know.

WAY 26   THINK ABOUT THE IMPLICATIONS

As you prepare your thoughts, think about the implications of your message. Although it may seem easier at the time, it is not always sensible to ad lib. When you do, it is easy to be so casual that you make promises you cannot keep. If it happens that you cannot deliver on your promises, you run the risk of letting people down. Suppose you are counselling an employee about absenteeism. You are deciding whether to let the person 'off the hook' or to discipline her. If you don't think in advance about the implications of that decision, you risk setting precedents that you may regret later.

The same is true for all the messages you send. Think about their implications. For instance, are there any economic implications to your ideas? What are they? Might you offend someone with your remarks? Are you revealing bias towards a particular group? Will you be perceived as pulling a flanker on your boss? Are you telling a half-truth?

Because managers are role models, consider whether you would be proud of others emulating you. Would you be embarrassed or angry if your subordinates imitated you? To avoid mis-communication, anger, frustration or embarrassment think about the implications of your messages.

WAY 27   ELIMINATE THE EXTRANEOUS

When you organize your thoughts, determine what is essential to your message and what is not. Eliminate the extraneous. Too often reports, conversations, memos and talks are filled with information designed to impress rather than to advance the arguments. The extra material may make the report appear weighty or the speaker sound important. However, wordiness can confuse what you want to present clearly. Such extra material is usually included because the speaker or the writer didn't take the time to eliminate what was unnecessary. Too often rough drafts or unrehearsed talks are presented as final ones. Unfortunately they read like rough drafts or sound like unrehearsed talks. When you know what you are communicating and why, then decide what you need to include to make your point. Certainly a good story or anecdote may lighten the moment, but if it isn't relevant, let it go.

It distracts.

In a report, if you have pages filled with charts and graphs, ask yourself what purpose each one serves. If they don't support or clarify your point, then don't use them. File them for future use. Put them in an appendix, so that readers can look at them without interrupting the flow of their reading. Stick to your point. Your audience will, too. What is true for reports is equally true for other forms of communication. Make your point clear by eliminating extraneous information.

WAY 28   ANTICIPATE OBJECTIONS

As you organize your thoughts, anticipate the arguments you are likely to hear. Expect people to say that they don't have the time, the money, the interest, the background or the personnel to implement your proposals. Your audience's organizational roles, hobby horses or particular biases vis-à-vis you or the company should help you identify some areas of contention and enable you to prepare for their arguments.

- Some may view your remarks as threatening to themselves or to one of their pet projects.
- Some may view your message as a threat to their authority rather than as an opportunity for development.
- Some may view your recommendations as too time-consuming or as non-essential to the effective running of the organization.

If you have studied your audience, you can anticipate objections. That way you can prepare your arguments or your answers in advance.

WAY 29   CREATE A STRUCTURE

Buildings have structures. Reports, talks and meetings need strong underpinnings, too. Analyse your message to see if it can be divided into segments. It is easier to take bites of a sandwich than to gulp it down whole. In the same way it is easier to comprehend the whole by understanding the parts. The basic structure includes a beginning, a middle and an end. The beginning sets the context or introduces the material. The middle develops the ideas.

The end restates your position.

Suppose you are preparing a series of recommendations. As you work on them, you notice that some relate to budget, others to staffing and still others to policy. Consider creating three categories with those headings – budgetary, staffing and policy – then fit your recommendations into each of them. In your introduction, explain that you will be making three kinds of recommendations – budgetary, staffing and policy. Thus, the audience is prepared to learn about the three kinds of recommendations. You have helped them follow your logic. As a result, they may more readily understand your arguments.

Don't forget the end. Don't forget to restate your point or message. Even in a chat, we make small talk, move to our point, but then need to conclude in some way to ensure that the message is clear. The most common structure is the tried and true beginning, middle and end.

WAY 30 ORDER YOUR INFORMATION

Well designed lengthy messages sequence information according to some pattern. Just as it is easier to remember a sentence than it is to recall a series of random words, it is easier for your audience to follow your thinking if there is a logical sequence. The pattern is your choice and depends on your message. Let's consider some patterns.

Order of importance. Present your most important ideas first, then the next most important and then the next. You might decide that reverse order is a better pattern in a particular instance, so put the most important item last. Most news programmes begin and close with headlines. Why? To keep our attention and because people tend to recall what they hear or see first.

Number. Tell the audience that you are going to make 1, 3, 5, 10 or 18 points in your presentation. Then, do say 'one', then 'two', then 'three' until you have gone over each of the items that you promised.

Chronology. Begin with what occurred in the past. Then continue with the present and conclude with the future. Reverse chronology is another option. That method involves discussing the present first and then going backwards in time.

Spatially. Organize your material so that your analysis moves from the left to the right, right to left, top to bottom, bottom to top, back to front, east to west, north to the south or big to small.

Mnemonics. Organize your ideas by using memory devices. To do that look at the key words in your message. Then take the first letter from each of those words and identify a single word made up of those letters that encapsulates what you are saying. For example, your four points might be H for Health, O for Opportunity, P for Purpose, E for Economics. Remember HOPE.

Opposites. Discuss all the negatives or all the disadvantages in one part of your presentation. Then group all the positives or advantages in another.

Which technique you use doesn't matter, but having one does. So, take the time to organize your thoughts. Remember sequencing helps the audience follow your thinking. It's particularly important when your message is complex or lengthy.

WAY 31 USE IMAGES

You have heard the expression, 'A picture is worth a thousand words'. It's true. Try to remember a talk you heard , a meeting you attended or some material you read. What comes to mind? Most of us can recall some image from the experience. You may remember the speaker touching his face, or a slide that the speaker used to make a point. Take that recollection to heart. What you recall is most likely what others do: pictures. But they need not be photographs. They can be verbal experiences, too. Therefore, when you prepare your communication, try to incorporate examples, images and analogies that are memorable.

- Can you compare a complex situation to something simpler?
- Can you describe a situation so the audience can visualize it?
- Can you put your numbers and statistics together in such a way that what emerges isn't just columns of numbers and figures?
- Can you create a pie chart? Can you show comparisons?
- Can you actually use an image rather than a line on the chart?

The more vivid your images, the more the audience will remember. Your objective is to have readers and listeners remember what you want them to recall, be it a recommendation, a reprimand, an appraisal or an update.

One caveat: be sure that your image is not more memorable than your message. Burst balloons or ride in on a donkey, if you wish, but will anyone remember what you said? Choose your images, but select them wisely.

Seven
Valuing People

Understanding your audience goes well beyond analysing demographic data. You are working with human beings. People have foibles. People are weak and strong. People have emotions. People have values. You cannot underestimate the importance for a communicator of being sensitive to people. The following set of ways addresses some human issues.

WAY 32   CONSIDER THE LOCATION

Conveying a message to colleagues in a pub is different from conveying the same message in a board room. Chatting with a colleague by the water cooler is different from making a presentation to 400 people in a conference. What is effective on a Friday afternoon may not work on a Monday morning. Conveying news about major organizational changes requires a different approach from giving a weekly status report. What is appropriate over cocktails might not work over coffee in the conference room. What works well in a memo might not work at all in a formal report. Consider your message and the setting for its presentation before deciding on the most appropriate tone. Typically, the more people you address in writing or orally the more formal you tend to be. Formality, however, does not mean stuffiness or high flown vocabulary. When the audience is larger or more remote, you have less information about the knowledge base or the personalities of all involved, so you can make fewer assumptions. Remember location affects your message.

WAY 33   TREAT PEOPLE WITH RESPECT

No matter how stressful the situation is that you are in, always treat people with respect and dignity. At times, you will have to deal with irate or frustrated colleagues or customers. Under stress, people may shout, rage or weep. Hopefully, you will have anticipated possible emotional reactions to negative news and you will have prepared for such responses. However, if you find yourself to be the subject of such an outburst, maintain your own dignity as well as that of the other person. Sometimes people may ask you questions that you believe to be stupid, posturing or belligerent.

- Allow your questioners to express their feelings in their own way, rather than letting your feelings be known.
- Listen, maintain your own decorum and take the question seriously. Know that, in fact, those people may not want answers. They may just want to get their own messages off their chests.
- Keep focused on your message.
- Repeat your main points, if necessary, but do not be drawn into a verbal fist fight.
- Agree to research a contentious point.
- Encourage the combatant to provide you with data at another time.

If they persist or become angry, they, not you, will lose the respect of any other listeners. You gain stature, because you remain calm under fire.

WAY 34   MAINTAIN YOUR OBJECTIVITY

It is easy to get caught up in the heat of an argument or to passionately defend a point of view. If you become involved in either situation, maintain an objective view of the larger picture. Keep your vision in mind. Remember what you want to achieve. If you don't, you can be easily embroiled in the problems of others. Stay focused on your message. Don't allow yourself to be side-tracked with others' emotional arguments that move you off your essential points. Stay on the issues at hand. Don't become emotional yourself. It is easy to become angered when others don't appear to be listening to you or are not taking your work seriously. Try not to. Keep reminding yourself what you want to accomplish. Salespeople face rejection daily, but to be successful they have to keep focused on the next sale. Good communicators do, too. Certainly afterwards reflect on what is being said to you, but during the debate keep your purpose in mind.

WAY 35 BE SENSITIVE

Good communicators, as we have seen, anticipate and are careful. You want to reach everyone in your audience. You do not want to lose anyone by being offensive.

You can offend some people with off-colour jokes and by stereotyping. Suppose you refer to a particular nationality as fat or loud, to seniors as decrepit, to consumers as gullible or teenagers as irresponsible, you risk offending someone. Not everyone in that country is fat or loud, not all seniors are decrepit, not all consumers are gullible, not all teenagers irresponsible. When individuals hear the remark, they think about it and you. They stop paying attention to your view of strategic marketing. You have lost them.

You can offend some people with your examples and your pronouns. If you want to create a sense of team, use 'we' instead of 'I'. Watch the use of 'he' and 'she'. Both men and women buy groceries and do the laundry. Men and women are corporate executives.

You can offend some people by making disparaging remarks. As you well know, people have strong feelings about the European Union, football, sexuality, divorce, politics and cloning, to name but a few. Be careful about what you say about them. You cannot be aware of every issue that might be emotive to someone. Be cautious about the possibilities of hurting people and thus losing them. Don't cast aspersions. Be sensitive to others' feelings.

WAY 36 AVOID OVER-GENERALIZING

All men do not play golf. All women do not knit. All industries are not the same either. Be sure that remarks you make about people or companies can be substantiated with hard data. You immediately recognize over-generalization, if a report suggests that all motor way deaths are caused by the drinks industry. When film and television are blamed for all teenage violence, you recognize another generalization. In the same way be sure that you are not over-generalizing and can prove your case when you identify the cause of an organizational problem. The same is true when you are convincing clients that 'all the problems' will go away if particular recommendations are implemented. Will 'all the problems' go away? Say only what you can support. If you are challenged and you cannot provide supporting data to make your case, you risk not only losing your argument but also your credibility.

Eight
Choosing Appropriate Words

Words are wonderful. We have thousands to select from when we communicate. In this book it is not possible to discuss all words or combinations of words, but we can suggest eight ways that should enhance your communication.

WAY 37   BE SPECIFIC

Avoid generalities. Don't say the meeting was 'marvellous', the report was 'splendid', the presentation was 'superb'. The meeting, the report, the presentation may have been all of these things but without specific supporting details these words are all too vague to be useful.

Write or speak about issues with specificity. Rather than indicating that there has been an 'upward trend in pricing', be specific. Describe the increase. Give the percentages. Rather than saying we will be 'cutting back' on lunch hours, say that we will be 'cutting back lunches by 5 minutes' or by '5 minutes once a week'.

When you are specific, your audience better grasps what you mean and can better evaluate the impact of your remarks on their work. In addition, they can remember your point.

Again, recall occasions when you have had difficulty understanding or knowing what to do because the communicator used too many abstractions. Identify the 'competitive advantage'? Explain the 'pressure' the organization is under. Clarify the 'strategy' you are recommending. If you are proud of someone's efforts, tell him or her why you are proud. If you are dissatisfied, say so. Be specific. Your words will be remembered.

WAY 38   USE EXAMPLES

An hotelier once described the view from the dining room window of his inn as 'beautiful'. A second hotelier described a view of fields of pink and yellow wild flowers, horses grazing and a rugged mountain rising sharply in the background. Both scenes may be 'beautiful'. But it is more memorable to describe exactly what you see out the window than saying that the view is 'beautiful'. How often have you read a brochure that uses words like 'luxurious', 'cozy' or 'comfortable'? What do those words mean? Is the room luxurious because of three inch deep carpeting or because it has a jacuzzi? Are there telephones and television in the bathroom? Whenever possible, use words to create pictures.

The same is true if you discipline employees or if you praise them. Don't threaten punishment, describe it. What will happen? We will have to 'take measures' if you don't submit your reports on time. Well, what 'measures'? Describe the measures as visually as possible.

Suppose you want to discuss the notion of 'overcoming objections'. Identify examples of objections to your product or service, then demonstrate how each one might be overcome. Clarify your points. If you don't, the audience will remain unsure of your meaning, because your discussion will be too theoretical.

WAY 39   MAKE ANALOGIES

When a message is too abstract or unclear for us, we may become bewildered, confused, frustrated or fatigued. When we do, we stop paying attention. We start thinking about other things. One of the best ways to keep the attention of others is to use examples or analogies that help clarify your complex point. Just as electronic mail uses terms like 'mailbox' to simplify the concept make analogies to experiences that we have around the house, the office or at the shop.

WAY 40   BE POLITICALLY AWARE

If you think that your message may cause distress or anxiety, be ready to handle some of the concerns that the audience as a whole or as individuals may have. For example, your message may be threatening. People may feel that your message will create too much work for them or that it will lessen their work load, creating too much or too little pressure. Your staff may be concerned about having to work with new people or in ways that are unfamiliar to them. As a consequence, they will feel insecure.

In addition, people with different job titles often have different perspectives on issues. A union representative may interpret your ideas differently than an accountant. The managing director's perspective may differ from that of the secretary to the board. In the same way, the reactions of newer board members may differ from those of more senior members. Anticipate how differing constituencies or individuals may interpret what you are communicating. Present your arguments with their concerns in mind. Be politically aware.

WAY 41   AVOID HYPERBOLE

Beware of exaggeration. Over-enthusiasm may cause you to exaggerate. It may lull you into making promises that you cannot keep. Beware of hyperbole. If you exaggerate or cannot keep a promise, you lose credibility.

We have all experienced the sales pitch which virtually tells us that a particular widget can clean our windows, dice our carrots and blow dry our hair. Fine, if it can perform that way. But if the widget cannot produce as promised, we, the consumers, will be disappointed. In the same way one over-blown statement may cause your entire message to be suspect. Catch yourself writing or using phrases that suggest that 'Everyone will be thrilled by the results of our work.' And stop yourself when you are about to say that 'Maura's decision will solve the problem' or that 'Paul's action was the cause...' Will everyone be thrilled? Will Maura's decision solve it? Was Paul's action the only reason? Be wary that your enthusiasm for a project may colour your thinking. While you want to be specific, you don't want to commit to what may not be true.

WAY 42   BE ACCURATE

Your audience has a right to expect accuracy. Be careful, therefore, of using an inaccurate statistic, of making an error on a graph, of presenting an invalid finding, or of using a wrong name. Errors lead to your undermining your own efforts to communicate successfully. Just one error could lead people to believe you may be guilty of more than one. So, be accurate.

Check and double check that the words or the images that you are using are the ones that accurately convey your ideas. If every room in your hotel has a window overlooking the sea, then you can say so. If only a third of them do, then you cannot say that all the rooms overlook the sea. If you know that the cost will be £200, then say £200 not £175. If you promised to phone a client the next day at 10 and have no intention of doing so, don't promise it. If you believe that your solution for a technical problem will make a difference to everyone in the organization, say so, but if you aren't sure, don't. Better yet, identify those areas in which your solution may help. You will be believed. Think about how you felt when you were misled.

WAY 43   RATION PET PHRASES

Over time, most of us develop pet phrases which we repeat. In small numbers, they are harmless. In fact, if your audience knows you well, they may even anticipate them. However, when you find that the audience is listening for those expressions rather than for the more important message that you might have, beware! Catch yourself using them.

- Suppose you use the same word over and over. For instance, Let's say that you say 'super' to describe your feelings about events. Do it too often and eventually your audience won't believe you when you use it.
- Suppose you misuse a word – 'irregardless' – and sprinkle it throughout your talk or your documents, its appearance will detract from the rest of your message.
- Suppose you overuse phrases and words like, 'you know', 'ok', 'like' or ' as such'.
- Suppose you use the same comparison or analogy over and over again. Did you ever wager with yourself or someone else on the frequency with which the phrase would be used at a meeting? People do.

No harm having phrases that you like. If they are overused be aware that they are distracting. Discover if you have any and then ration their use.

WAY 44   MAINTAIN CONFIDENTIALITY

If you violate confidentiality, you lose the trust and respect of others. Such a loss is costly. It is said that our names and reputations are our most precious possessions. That refers to your own name and to the name of your company as well. Some information is to be safeguarded and not to be shared. So, if you violate confidentiality, you lose the trust and respect of others.

When you counsel an employee about a problem and agree that the discussion will remain confidential, then you should honour your agreement. Don't reveal proprietary information to competitors. If you have completed research that should not be shared, don't share it. Sometimes maintaining confidentiality can be difficult to do, particularly when you have been immersed in a project. Because you have been living with the project for so long, it is easy to forget that your material may not be appropriate for everyone's ears or eyes. Once again, think carefully about your audience. Be sure that you are communicating only what is appropriate for everyone who might have access to your thoughts. Be careful of what you write and just as careful of what you say.

Nine

Using your Non-Verbal Behaviour

Don't forget that we communicate non-verbally, too. Good communicators are sensitive to the impact their non-verbal behaviour can have on others. As you well know, many of our first impressions are formed long before another person speaks to us.

WAY 45   USE YOUR FACE AND HANDS

Our faces and hands are expressive. Hands in particular are a valuable and available pair of visuals:

- you can lift your hands;
- you can count on your fingers;
- you can use your hands to describe shapes;
- you can heft imaginary weight;
- you can make a fist; avoid pointing, however – it's rude and threatening;
- you can open and close your hands.

Rather than jamming your hands into your pockets, putting them behind your back or fiddling with paper, pens or pencils, use them to describe. Hands are expressive and can reinforce your message dramatically.

Your face, too, is a wonderful visual. Like your hands, your face can convey a message just as your words do. Even when you are listening, your face conveys a message:

- we can raise or knit our eyebrows;
- we can turn the corners of our mouths up or down;
- we can drop our jaws;
- we can frown, smile, look quizzical, thoughtful, angry and bewildered.

101 WAYS TO BETTER COMMUNICATION

Rather than be expressionless, use your face. If you are pleased, smile. If you are concerned, frown. Your face should mirror your words, not contradict them. When you say you are 'delighted to meet' someone, you should appear to be delighted. If you are concerned about third quarter profits then you should look concerned not happy.

Don't underestimate the impact of your hands and your face.

WAY 46 USE YOUR VOICE

Most people have good voices. Few of us take full advantage of what our voices can do:

- you can raise or lower your voice;
- you can whisper;
- you can laugh;
- you can speak swiftly or slowly.

Varying your tone of voice when you speak makes what you are saying more interesting to the listener. Ever been bored by someone who droned on at the same pitch and pace? Monotones are boring. Perhaps you've noticed others in the room actually nodding off when someone drones on. Speeding up, slowing down, raising or lowering your voice helps maintain interest in your remarks. In addition, by making changes in your delivery, you can emphasize significant sections or de-emphasize material that is less critical. Stop from time to time, too. Pausing is a wonderful technique. It gives people time to absorb what you are saying. In addition, it can underline an important point. People are startled by silence.

Voices have different qualities. Some people are soft-spoken, others bellow. Some people have strong regional accents that are musical but may be difficult for a stranger to understand. Get to know your own voice better. Record yourself on tape.

Learn to modulate your voice in different circumstances. If you have a powerful voice and are speaking in a small room, lower your volume. If you are soft-spoken and are talking in a large room, don't assume you need a mike, try slowing down. You don't have to shout. When we are nervous, most of us speak too quickly. If you catch yourself rushing, consciously slow down. If

44

you decide to record yourself, listen for any extraneous noises that you may make. Do you hear 'um' or 'er'? Do you smack your lips together? Remember there's nothing wrong with those noises until your listeners notice them to the exclusion of what you are saying. Using your voice and face well is another way to enhance your ability to communicate.

WAY 47   EXAMINE YOUR POSTURE

If you don't have a video camera, find a full-length mirror and stand before it as if you were going to give a talk. Move around. Take a close look at yourself. Do you normally stand tall with shoulders squared and hips parallel to the floor? Or are your shoulders and hips all akimbo? If they are, then you may appear coquettish or cowboy-like. You should look natural, not like a stick figure or a totem pole. You want to stand tall with your head up. When you do, you can take more air into your lungs. This enables you to project your voice further. By the way, if you are nervous, taking deep breaths has a calming effect.

Look at your feet. Do you normally rock backward and forward on your toes? Do you bounce? Do you take small dance steps? Catch yourself if you do. If you don't, people may focus more on what you are doing with your feet than they do on your message.

Now walk. When you are speaking don't be afraid to move around the room. A mobile figure can be more interesting than a static one. We are not talking about pacing back and forth like a caged lion. Move naturally. Walk, stop, get close to some people then walk toward others. The proximity enables you to see reactions better. Also, if you tend to speak quickly, walking slows your delivery. Study your posture.

WAY 48   KNOW YOUR IDIOSYNCRASIES

Idiosyncrasies distract your audience and detract from your message. Just as you may have the habit of repeating pet phrases, you may also have gestures that you overuse. Like overused words, when an action is repeated too often in a short period of time, your audience focuses more on your gesture than they will on what you are saying.

- Ever see people keep tossing their heads trying to keep wayward strands of hair behind their ears?
- Ever know people who constantly smooth their ties?
- Ever see people keep nervous fingers busy by playing with a button, the edge of a hem or with keys and coins in their pockets? They tap a pencil, twist a ring or fiddle with paper.
- Ever see people rock back and forth or up and down?
- Ever see people push their glasses up their noses only to have them slip again, requiring a new push?
- Ever meet people who constantly clear their throats, rub their ears or twirl their hair?

By themselves, each of these behaviours and activities is innocuous. Repeated too often, they will be noticed, and people will count them. It might be a good idea to ask a friend or a colleague if you have any such habits. If you do, eliminate them.

Ten
Improving your Image

This section is about your image. How you project yourself as a business person has an impact on others. You may be perceived as professional or unprofessional by the way you look and act. Such judgements may be fair or unfair, but your image is a factor in doing business.

WAY 49   LOOK AT YOURSELF

In Way 47 you were advised to study yourself in a mirror or video-tape to learn how you stand and move. Look again. Look at your-self from top to toe. How do you appear? Do you dress appropriately for the job you have? Are you neat? Do your clothes fit? Are your collars, cuffs, and hems the right length? Are your clothes clean, or is there a spot of coffee on your tie or are there ink smudges on your cuffs? Even on 'dress down' days, are your clothes pressed? Are your shoes shined? While shined shoes may not be appropriate for work on construction sites, you can still look neat. Perhaps you are expected to wear a uniform in your job. Is it clean and pressed? Does it look as if you threw it on a chair the night before? Are shirts or blouses tucked in? Is your hair cut to suit the occasion, or do you have a style which makes your hair cover your eyes? Are you wearing clothing that might be construed as provocative? Are you wearing patterns or combinations of colours that are shocking?

Like idiosyncratic words, sounds or gestures, you don't want your clothing to command more attention than your ideas.

- If you are wearing a plunging neckline, a startling tie or 4 inch dangling earrings that are distracting, then you have made an unwise choice.
- If you are wearing perfume or aftershave that is so powerful

that people stand back from you, then you have made an unwise choice.

- If you are wearing shoes that don't fit well or make your feet hurt, then you have also made an unwise choice.
- If you not wearing glasses, because you are too vain, but you can't see without them, you have made an unwise choice.

Look at yourself and consider how you would look to a prospective client, boss or a new colleague.

WAY 50   EXAMINE YOUR OFFICE

You have just taken a hard look at yourself. Now do the same for your office. True, we all work differently. Some of us like to have desks with nothing on them. Others of us have desks covered with books, diskettes, files and papers. Whichever way you prefer to work, you should be able to find what you are seeking with ease.

Look at your desk. Do you see any confidential files lying around? Are phone messages and unopened mail strewn around your desk? Do you have notes lying around carelessly that should have been filed or thrown away? Are there crumpled papers? Are there overheads from presentations from two years ago? Are there dated samples?

Look at the walls. Do you have photographs or framed sayings that might offend others? If you have a calendar, is the current month showing? Do you have an ego wall covered with your awards and degrees, diplomas and certificates? Do you need them all? Who are they for – you or for the person who comes into your office? What kind of pictures do you have? Why? What effect would they have on others?

Look around. Do you have old coffee cups, drink cans, or empty water bottles strewn about? Are greasy paper bags or yoghurt containers from old lunches lying around? Are papers coffee-stained? If this is a broad picture of your office, consider the impression that it might make on another person. While you may think that all that paper makes you look busy, a visitor may perceive you to be careless, disorganized, understaffed or sloppy.

In addition, note how you have arranged your office. Is it friendly? If people want to talk to you, can they sit somewhere? How are chairs positioned? Across the desk from you? Beside your desk? Do you always talk to people while you are sitting behind your desk and thus appear protected or unapproachable? Do you sit around a small table?

Look at your desk, your walls, your work and recognize that they project an image of you. Ask yourself, if it is the one you want.

WAY 51   EXAMINE YOUR PAPERWORK

Let's take a look at what leaves your office with your name on it. Does it reflect the way you want to be seen.? Think about how your paperwork appears. When you give a talk, what do you use for notes? A page torn from a refill pad or note cards? When you take a phone message, do you write it on a pad? Or do you write on the handiest white space available, even if it is the budget or a formal report?

While large organizations may have a corporate logo and official letterhead, small companies may not. Either way, think about how documents that are produced by your office appear to other people. Do all the outgoing letters look different, or do they have the same format? In other words, you may want letters, memos and reports to look alike. While the content will differ, the format will not. Consider developing a 'house style'. Having one means that you have determined the lay out, font, spacing, headings, bullets, use of white space, cover page, binders and binding. That effort at consistency should create professional looking documents.

WAY 52   BE COURTEOUS

Little things do mean a lot especially when you are dealing with people in business. People remember the graciousness of others or their lack of it. People value 'Good morning', 'Good-bye', 'Thank you' and 'Please'. But courtesy means more than saying 'Please' and 'Thank you'.

- Have you ever been yawned at over the telephone?
- Have you ever been kept on hold and nobody ever came back to see if you were still waiting or to say thank you for holding?
- Have you ever been kept on hold and been thanked for holding?

In one instance you may become frustrated; in another, you are made to feel important to the caller and the company. Big companies with telephone menus are making phoning more impersonal and frustrating for the caller. But every phone call, every letter is important.

- Have you ever applied for a position, sent in a CV and then never heard another word? It's amazing what a brief note indicating the status of your application can do for an applicant's attitude toward a company.
- Have you ever sent a memo seeking feedback and received none?
- Have you ever covered the reception desk and been ignored by colleagues who walk by?
- Have you ever joined into a small group of people and have no one take responsibility for making introductions?

Never be in too much of a hurry to remember the courtesies. When people do something for you, don't take it for granted. Do say thank you. A personal touch matters to others. When you indicate that you will get back to someone with information in a week's time, it is common courtesy to do what you promised. In a week's time phone or send a note providing what you promised or indicating that there will be a delay. You are respecting other people's dignity when you are polite. And these are just some of the little things that mean so much. You could make your own list.

WAY 53   EXAMINE YOUR COMPANY'S IMAGE

For the most part, we have been focusing on you as an individual. But you are part of an organization and that organization should appear as attractive and professional as well as its individual members do.

What does your company communicate? To answer this question we must go beyond the attractive brochures and the expensive logo. Take a walk. Pretend you are a visitor. Look at the street outside or your parking area, the entrance or the reception desk. What is the first thing you see? Are windows and doors clean? Are signs clear and attractive? When you enter what do you see? Old newspapers and magazines, old coffee cups, ashtrays filled with sweet wrappers? Are the plants looking wilted or are they cared for? Is the receptionist courteous with everyone or with just the so-called important people? Are visitors greeted with a smile and, made comfortable or are they ignored? Is the office dirty and dusty looking? Do the people in the office have long faces or are they pleasant looking? Are bins full? Do employees smile and greet strangers, or are they too self-absorbed? Are lavatories available and clean?

Sloppy offices and poor attitudes suggest sloppy and poor attitudes toward others and possibly toward work. Remember to look for the messages that your organization sends. Your corporate image can turn off your audience.

Organizations can alienate audiences.

- Ever have someone be rude because you were put through to a wrong extension?
- Ever been asked to wait in a reception area only to find two and three month old magazines or old coffee cups? Meanwhile the receptionist chats loudly about personal matters.

If letters are grammatically incorrect, if offices are sloppy or employees rude, your perception of the company will be negative.

Eleven
Getting Feedback

Unfortunately we think that we are being criticized when we are given information about our behaviour or our performance. People interpret the word, 'criticism', to be harmful and hurtful. But in reality, more often than not, feedback provides opportunities for us to develop and enhance our abilities. Welcome feedback.

WAY 54   LISTEN, LISTEN, LISTEN

Feedback lets you know what people like, dislike, need or want. It keeps you and your company informed. It provides valuable data you can get in few other ways.

If you are told or if you hear that a report or talk was too long, too convoluted, or too confusing, weigh the information. Suppose you hear that a particular team is not working together. Find out why and apply what you learn to improve their work. While you may consider that the work was well-done, consider the opinions of others. Listening is one way to obtain feedback about what you write or about what you say and about what others write or say.

Listen for general comments, too. People express their likes and dislikes. They indicate what they find difficult to deal with or what they resent. If your associates indicate that they dislike being kept in the dark or are confused by conflicting information, they will say so. If secretaries say that their bosses never tell them where they are going, you have information not only about what secretaries prefer but also about what managers ought to do. If you hear people express their disappointment because their opinions are never sought, then you know another way to alleviate unhappiness.

Listen, listen, listen. Reflect on what you hear and then consider acting on it or incorporating the information into your own communication style.

WAY 55   ASK QUESTIONS

You can sit in a meeting, in the cafeteria or walk down the corridor and overhear what people are saying, but being assertive about acquiring information helps, too. Ask questions. Ask others for their opinions. What did they think of your talk? What did they think about the recommendations that you made? Did they read your memo? What was their reaction to what you wrote? Ask them why they rejected your idea. What didn't they understand? Who was the best speaker at the conference? Why? In other words, seek information about your work.

Some organizations appraise their employees on a regular basis. Others don't. If your company uses a formal appraisal system and communication isn't a category for discussion then ask for a supervisor's opinion.

If your organization doesn't have formal evaluations, you may want to chat with your supervisor to get feedback on what you are doing well and what needs changing. Do the same for the people you supervise. Be sure that your own staff doesn't perceive your words as criticism. They should understand that you are directing them toward excellence. Do the same for the people you supervise. People feel more secure and more motivated when they are told what they are doing well and what needs improving. Without specific information, we operate in the dark. We may be making assumptions about the correct procedures to follow or worrying needlessly about failing to meet expectations.

Actively seek information – asking questions will give you added insights.

WAY 56   REFLECT

If you are listening to others and diligently asking questions, you can collect data about your communication style by sifting through that feedback. Arrive at your own conclusions. If you hear the same feedback often, then consider that it may be valid.

Suppose you learn from several people that you cannot always be heard clearly. It would surely mean that you need to speak up. If people phone your office seeking clarification of your memo, consider their calls feedback. Apparently what you wrote wasn't clear. To avoid the problem in the future, reread your memo to see what caused the confusion. Apply what you learn to your next piece of writing. Some of what you hear may be irrelevant. Some may be insightful. Whatever the case, try not to treat the information as hurtful. See it as useful.

And don't assume that only management has valuable insights. Different people in different jobs have different perspectives. Solicit their opinions and think about what they say. Even a minor change may enable you or your organization to be more effective. Reflect on what you learn and incorporate appropriate changes.

Part Two: Types of Communication

This section is devoted to improving specific types of communication activities. Although we have talked in general terms about speaking and writing, this section offers more specific ways of improving your ability to run meetings, give presentations, write and interview.

Twelve
Conducting Meetings

Because we have all attended meetings that have lulled us into a stupor, many of us groan at the very thought of attending them. A memo or an e-mail message invites us to one, and we dread the prospect of wasting our time. However, meetings can be important and valuable opportunities to share ideas. Meetings provide opportunities to clarify issues, educate and brainstorm. Too often, when we want to talk about an issue, we catch people on the fly rather than having a scheduled time to sit uninterrupted and talk. Meetings are opportunities to share ideas, to argue reasonably and to interact. You and your colleagues benefit from well-run meetings. Don't underestimate their value.

WAY 57   HAVE AN AGENDA

Well-run meetings usually have prepared agendas. What is an agenda? It is a plan. It consists of a list of items in the order that they are to be discussed. One of the advantages of using an agenda is the very act of putting it together. The process involves your thinking through the items in advance of the meeting and then prioritizing them. If you send a copy of your agenda to the other attendees in advance of the meeting, you give them the opportunity to prepare for it. Having the opportunity to reflect on issues may improve the quality of the discussion. Some of us need more reflective time than others. Therefore, rather than having everyone react spontaneously to a question like, 'What do you think of the proposal?' individuals will have been able to think about questions or concerns and to have brought supporting data with them.

Some meetings have one item on the agenda; others have as many as 17 or more. When setting your agenda, be realistic. Think about whether one item might be so contentious that it could warrant an entire meeting or that attempting to discuss 17 items is unrealistic given the amount of time. In the case of a long list, perhaps two 45 minute meetings at two different times would permit the participants to concentrate on all the issues. Minds wander when meetings run too long. Prepare an agenda.

WAY 58   MANAGE TIME

We're used to learning that an upcoming meeting '…is on Friday at 9:00', or '…will be on Tuesday at 2:30'. In addition to giving the start time for the meeting, consider indicating the ending time, too. You could say that the meeting will be 'an hour long', that it 'will run from 9:00 to 10:30' or that it will 'not adjourn before noon'. Having that information enables your colleagues to arrange their own schedules and adjust their workloads. Some may have to clear calendars, others may have to reschedule a meeting or phone calls. Your own meetings will be more productive if the participants aren't looking at their watches, stepping out to make phone calls, or apologizing for leaving. When people are preoccupied with their own obligations, they will not be concentrating on the issues at hand. In addition, by giving them the approximate length of the meeting, they will appreciate your sensitivity to their work loads. One caveat: if you do call a half hour meeting or an hour and a half meeting, abide by that time. Keep an eye on your watch or on the clock.

WAY 59   MAINTAIN ORDER

Unless you control discussions, meetings can get out of hand. When they do, your agenda and your time schedule go by the boards. It happens occasionally because some people like to hear the sound of their own voices or enjoy bringing in extraneous issues. Concentrate on the issues being discussed. When discussion becomes protracted, bring it back to the subject rather than let the talk wander far afield. Suppose the issue of this week's meeting is this year's training budget for the personnel department. Be sure that the discussion is about that, not about last year's training budget, next year's annual picnic, training policies in general or the finance department's carpet. Keep your colleagues on your topics, not their own. To rein them in:

- you can thank them for their enthusiasm and commitment;
- you can point out that you have a limited amount of time;
- you can recommend that the new issues are important enough to raise at another meeting;
- you can ask those concerned to provide the information and distribute it to the others present.

In other words, without denigrating individuals who tend toward lengthy explanations or presentations, stop them. If you don't, you will not meet your objectives and you will waste company time. Even if you are not using formal parliamentary rules, you need to control the process. One way to lose support is to have asked someone to prepare a report for a meeting and then have to exclude it because the discussion of other issues has taken too long.

WAY 60   ENCOURAGE INVOLVEMENT

Certainly discourage individuals who use your meetings as forums to discuss their own personal issues. With careful handling you can control people who attempt to dominate all discussions. Unfortunately some people view meetings as opportunities to promote themselves or to denigrate others. While reining in those people, you may also want to encourage more reticent people to participate. Be sensitive to the fact that not everyone thinks quickly or speaks comfortably at meetings. Some people are more reflective than others or are less willing to express their opinions. Being new to the organization or to the issues may cause others to be reluctant to speak. The power structure may be a deterrent to others. Bullying or sarcastic behaviour may discourage still others. When you chair meetings, be aware of who is participating and who is not. Encourage everyone to add their thoughts. Invite comments. Ask direct questions. While some people may be uncomfortable speaking, by asking them to, you are indicating that you value their insights.

Don't use the technique of calling on each person in turn around the table. Knowing their turn is coming, people may stop listening to others in order to prepare their own thoughts. They will not hear what the person two seats to their right has said. Having spoken, they will relax, relieved that they are 'off the hook'.

Another method for encouraging involvement is to invite the

participants to recommend items for the agenda in advance of the meeting. People will feel that their opinions are valued, because they will have been asked to be part of the process. And they will be less likely to complain about the issues being discussed when they are given the opportunity to offer suggestions and have declined to participate.

WAY 61 KEEP A RECORD

We've indicated that meetings are valuable opportunities for sharing ideas. Too often, however, good ideas are praised at the time, but then forgotten. So as not to lose them, record key ideas, concerns and actions. While records are usually kept at formal meetings, not all meetings are formal. Nevertheless, it is important in an informal setting to remember what has been said and by whom. If someone volunteered to research an answer, to follow up on a question, to form a committee, or to report back at a subsequent meeting, those decisions should be recorded. If a brilliant notion is introduced but there is no time for discussion, it would be criminal to forget the idea because no one had the foresight to take notes.

It doesn't matter whether you, a colleague or a secretary take the minutes, but someone should keep a record. Too many good ideas are lost because of the absence of minutes. Too many meetings rehash previously resolved issues because no one wrote down the thoughts at the time. And when there is no record, people may not be held accountable for their responsibilities. Minutes should be written up quickly following a meeting. The longer they remain as notes, the more likely it is that the typed minutes will differ markedly from the original discussion, simply because memory fades.

Thirteen
Giving Presentations

Talking one-to-one in business with someone is an everyday occurrence. So is speaking to groups. The latter, however, is more daunting. You feel alone and vulnerable. No matter how well prepared you are, you always have a nagging sense that disaster may befall you or that you may make a fool of yourself. Because we are making presentations frequently, let's look at some ways to make them less frightening and more effective. Let's reduce that sense of impending disaster we know all too well.

WAY 62   KNOW THE VENUE

Many speakers walk into a room just in time to speak. As a result they may look bewildered, wonder where the microphone is, fiddle inexpertly with the volume controls. They do everything to make themselves look unprepared. It would be better to get to know the facilities. No matter how busy you are, arrange your schedule so that you can get into the room at least five or ten minutes ahead of time. If you are planning to use equipment, you will need more time.

Speaking of equipment: be sure you have what you need and check to be sure that it is working. If you are using a screen, have you tested one of your slides or transparencies on it? Do you need an extension cord? Will you trip over any wires that may be on the floor? Can the audience see you if you stand behind the lectern? Do you want to use one? Would you rather use a table instead? Does the lighting work? Where are the switches? Is the room so dark that you cannot see your notes, or so bright that the images on the screen appear indistinct?

While you are at it, check the acoustics. Are you walking on a wooden floor? Does it echo? Or do heavy curtains and thick carpets absorb sound? Do you have enough paper for your flip chart? Do you have markers? Do they have ink in them? Is there another event next door that might interfere with what you are doing? Are workers hammering? Is music playing? Is a party in progress? Where are the doors? Are there telephones that may ring while you are speaking? Do you have water to drink? How are the seats arranged? Look around. The more familiar you are with the room you will be using, the more comfortable you will be with the situation. You will also have anticipated and prepared for problems. If any of these potential problems are likely to interfere with your presentation, seek out the person in charge of the venue and have him or her resolve them before it is too late. You will also appear more confident to the audience.

WAY 63   TIME YOURSELF

Practise your talk. If at all possible, practise it in the room where you will be speaking. The more familiar you are with the placement of the chairs, the feel of the carpet, the sight angles, the extraneous sounds, the possible interruptions, the more at ease you will be. If you cannot access the room for as long as you want it, find some other place to rehearse. Run through your talk a number of times, timing yourself. Deliver your talk aloud rather than reading it to yourself. You'll notice that the time needed for reading a speech and speaking it out loud differ, so remember to build in time for laughter, for pauses and for slides or overheads. Build in the time the audience needs if they are watching a video.

Suppose you have 15 minutes to speak, then your talk should last 15 minutes, not 20. If you have 30 minutes, then your talk should last 30 minutes, not 35 or 45. If you will be taking questions, have you allowed enough time for them? How many will you take? Will you be taking them from the floor or will someone else handle them? Know if you are going to be introduced and what you want to be said about you or about the content of your talk.

The more you plan and practise, the less stressful the task becomes. Having someone else tell you that time is up detracts from your performance. Time yourself.

WAY 64 USE NOTE CARDS

Some people speak extemporaneously with ease. Most of us, however, cannot. We are nervous or afraid of appearing foolish. Some of us think that we will black out, faint or forget everything that we know. To overcome those perfectly normal feelings, prepare note cards. Having note cards reduces anxiety and makes you appear more professional. Note cards are actual cards, not sheets of refill paper. Have you ever seen a speaker walk to the lectern, reach into a pocket and pull out and unfold a sheet of paper? Is that professional looking? While the speech that followed may have included some novel ideas, crumpled papers surely gave the appearance of a rushed job. Audiences want to feel valued. They do not want to feel as if they were an afterthought.

- Notes on cards are easier to handle than notes on paper.
- Holding 3 x 5 cards in your hand is also easier than holding long sheets of paper.
- Cards eliminate the need for a lectern. You can move about the speaker's area with confidence.
- Cards enable you to gesture, to keep your head up and eyes forward rather than having to look down and read.

What is on your note cards? Essentially they hold the outline of what you are going to say.

- Each card holds a cue or point for you to remember.
- Cards should have the first few sentences written out completely because you are most nervous at the beginning. Have them – just in case.
- Cards should be numbered sequentially in case you drop them.

If you have never used cards before, they take some practise. Once you are used to them, you can keep them in a pocket and practise at different times of the day and in different locations.

Some people feel that they can work without any notes at all, but that may be too much of a risk for many of us. Even the most talented people can become nervous in an important situation and develop a block. Notes are your security blanket.

WAY 65   BE ENTHUSIASTIC

Think about the speakers you have seen and heard over the years. Compare those speakers who were animated about their subjects with those who seemed bored or uninterested. You will have noted that it is usually easier to listen to people who are enthusiastic. Why? Because their energy is contagious.

When you want people to listen to you, the more excited you can be about your subject, the more they will hang on your words. Your tone of voice, the look on your face, your emphasis and your body language all project enthusiasm. Do you look and sound as if you are delivering a eulogy? Do you smile? Do your eyes light up? Do you exude energy? Or do you look as if you need a transfusion? Let your audience see that you are delighted to be speaking to them, that you care about them and about your subject. Concentrating on a speaker for a long time isn't easy. Frankly, if you don't care about your subject, why should your audience?

WAY 66   MAINTAIN EYE CONTACT

Whether you are talking to one person, or delivering a speech to 400, or running a meeting of 20, try to look at everyone in your audience. When you look directly at the audience, you appear open and honest. You are indicating that you have nothing to hide. We have all seen speakers who look at the floor, at the ceiling, at their notes or at the wall in the back over the audience's heads – anywhere but at us. Are they bored? Are they hiding something? No matter how nervous you are, look at your audience. The same is true when you answer a question. Talk to everyone in the room, not just to the person who asked the question.

Another reason to look at the audience is to gauge their reactions. By looking at them, you can react to what you are seeing and make adjustments. Are people leaning forward trying to hear you? Are people squinting at your visuals? Are people smiling? Are they frowning? A quizzical expression on someone's face might suggest that you need to clarify your remarks by repeating what you have just said. A nodding head or heavy lids may suggest that people are tired or bored. You may have to adjust your presentation. Cut part of your talk. Speak more quickly through certain points. Change the pitch of your voice. Stop. Tell a story. Maintaining eye contact allows people to look at you and for you to see them. Be careful to talk to everyone, not only to the person who appears to be hanging on every word and nodding, or to the perceived decision maker.

Look at everyone. Talk to everyone. Everyone matters.

WAY 67   USE VISUALS

Listening is difficult. Our minds drift away from even the most exciting speaker because we can think faster than a speaker can talk. In addition, using only our ears to absorb information is not easy. Using other senses helps. That is one reason many of us take notes when someone speaks: most of us remember more when we both see and hear. Helping people retain information is one reason for using visuals. Another reason for using them is to clarify our message.

What is a visual? Visuals take many forms. They may be photographs, maps, blueprints, hand signals or facial expressions. They may also be papers you distribute. Visuals can be words, too. Metaphors and similes assist you in presenting ideas. You choose visuals that are appropriate for your message. Just be sure that the images you select assist the audience in remembering your words, rather than confusing them.

WAY 68   PREPARE FOR QUESTIONS

Questions don't suddenly materialize at the conclusion of a talk. Expect them and prepare for them, carefully. Your topic may be complicated or even startling to the audience. They may not be as familiar with it as you are, so they will probably need clarification. If they have knowledge of your topic, they may disagree with your rationale. In either case, they will have questions.

How do you prepare? You prepare for questions based on your knowledge of the audience. Assess the possibility of differing points of view on your subject. Perspectives on issues differ from department to department and from person to person. In addition, people have their own agendas. As you prepare, anticipate questions that people with differing perspectives or agendas might ask.

Prepare answers. Keep them simple and to the point. Consider having a colleague ask you some questions on your topic.

On the day, if you are confronted with a difficult question, and you don't know the answer, admit it. Don't waffle a response that you will regret later. If you are unsure about giving an answer on the spot, you can always say that you will look into the issue. You can also offer to get the information to the questioner at a later date.

With a hostile audience questioning can get tough. Don't lie. Don't blame. Assume responsibility. Stay on the point of your talk. Restate what you have said. Take the moral high ground. Avoid fighting with antagonistic members of the audience. If they persist, they, not you, will usually look bad and lose in the encounter. However, if you climb into the ring with them, you risk damaging your own credibility.

WAY 69   CONTROL YOUR NERVES

Being nervous is normal; just don't succumb to it. Expect to experience stage fright. When speaking, consider yourself an actor. The more you rehearse, the more you know your 'stage' or venue, the more confident you will be. The more confident you are, the less nervous you will be. Know your audience and know your lines. The more prepared you are, the more secure you should be, because practice decreases the level of uncertainty. However, expect to be nervous, particularly at the outset.

Get to know your own brand of nervousness. We all have our own patterns. Do you sweat or feel faint? Do your palms get wet? Do your hands shake? Does your neck turn red? Do you lose your voice? Do you frequently clear your throat? Do your legs feel heavy or weak? Do you have butterflies in your stomach? Does your heart pound? If so, what can you do to control your nerves?

- Avoid caffeine before a talk. Instead, drink room temperature water.
- Stand tall and take deep breaths. When you begin, which is when you are most nervous, speak very slowly. Remember that the first minute or two is the worst. After that you will calm down. So, anticipate that initial anxiety.
- Consider ways of taking attention off yourself at the beginning. Some speakers show slides or write on the flip chart so

that the audience focuses on the image. Others ask the audience a question.

- Recall calming images – a lake, the sky, the beach.
- Remind yourself that you have something valuable to share with the audience. You are making a difference.

Your nervousness will go, but it will come back the next time you speak. It is an adrenaline rush that gives you an edge and helps to make your speech a good one.

WAY 70   BE A TEAM PLAYER

At times you may be required to make a joint presentation. If that should occur, prepare together. If you do, you will look polished.

During the presentation itself team members who are not speaking should have their eyes glued on the ones who are and listen actively to what their colleagues are saying. One reason is to be sure that you can cover in case a colleague errs. Another one is because you are modelling the behaviour you want the audience to have. You want them to listen and react to what they are hearing, also. If you are looking around the room or chatting with a colleague, you are distracting the audience and suggesting by your actions that what is being said isn't important. You know it is. Your attitude should tell the audience that it is.

When you and your colleagues do your planning, decide on who is going to say what and in what order. The nature of the material should create its own logical divisions. Decide on who is going to handle the introductions, the order and the questions or certain types of questions. You may also have to agree on who will help with the equipment. For example, one person may advance the slides or change the transparencies while another speaks. A team presentation is just that: an opportunity for a group to demonstrate that they work well together to achieve their goals.

Fourteen
Writing for Business

In your role as a business person, you write letters, proposals, grants, reports, minutes, notes, e-mails, press releases or newsletters. Writing for business should be clear and to the point. It is not intended for relaxation or entertainment. Read John Grisham or Ruth Rendell for that. Business writing, on the other hand, should communicate ideas clearly to ensure success.

WAY 71   FIND THE TIME

Writing takes time. One reason business writing is not as good as it could be is because we do not dedicate enough time to it. Much of what we do write is completed under pressure. While we may produce good work, we don't always take the time to produce superior work. Too often, when we write memos, reports, letters or e-mails, we distribute what are, in fact, rough drafts. We don't build time into our days to reread or rewrite what we have written so as to ensure that our words accurately and clearly convey our messages. Instead, we work to the deadline.

Think about how you write. Do you allot blocks of time for writing or do you fit it in between other activities? Look at your diary or organizer. Do you have specific times for writing? We jot down times for appointments, meetings or phone calls. So, why can't we jot down times for writing? Note 9:00 phone calls, 11:00 meeting with Mr. Jones, 11:30–12:30 draft speech. Then allot another time slot for rewriting that speech.

Yes, writing requires rewriting. We know when we write passionate letters that we are supposed to put them under our pillows and reread them in the morning. We know that in the light of day our feelings and words may seem inappropriate. At least they should be more temperate. The same is true for most writing, not just for love or hate letters. Put your work under an imaginary pillow. Give it a few hours, overnight or a few days to sit. Give yourself some distance. Then reread what you have written and modify it. Build rewriting into your calendars. Clarity in writing facilitates the work of others and minimizes the amount of time that you spend explaining what you meant in the first place. That extra rewrite will make a difference in the reactions and responses that you get.

WAY 72   REMEMBER THE AUDIENCE

Writing is a solitary experience. We write in solitude, at home, in our cubicles, on a plane or in our offices. While we may very well be alone with our own thoughts, we must not forget that we are writing for an audience. We are writing for other people who have thoughts, experiences and feelings. When we speak face-to-face we can see immediate reactions. However, when we write that reaction may be days away or it may never come. The reader is not in the room with you. The reader may be miles away and unable to turn to you and ask what you meant by that last sentence or by the previous paragraph. Therefore, we have to keep the reader in our minds when we write. We have to imagine those people. We have to think about what they know and don't know. We have to write as clearly as possible for them.

WAY 73   REMEMBER THE DISTRIBUTION

Writing is also indelible. When you write, you create a record. After the fact, you can't say, 'Oops, I didn't mean to write that', or 'Disregard page 4'. Because writing is a record, think not only about the audience in general but also about the specific readers. Consider who gets the original document and who else might be given copies. Be sure that you haven't written anything that might be misconstrued or that faults someone. Know the distribution. By the way, be sure to include everyone who belongs on the list. Don't exclude anyone. When distributing written work, we can make errors of commission or omission. We can hurt or anger people by forgetting to give them a copy and bewilder others by including them when they shouldn't be.

Be particularly careful with the internet. I recall an incident when someone sent an e-mail to a colleague expressing her anxiety about a proposed candidate for a key management position. The writer meant to send it only to a colleague. In her rush, she sent the message to everyone in her division. Besides being embarrassed, she spent a lot of time explaining her intent. Because e-mail addresses are assortments of numbers and letters, mistakes are easy. Be equally careful about what you write in memos, letters or reports. If uncensored words fall into the wrong hands, ask yourself who might be surprised, offended or angered. What's your relationship with that person? Will you lose credibility?

As you have before, think about the implications, when you distribute your writing.

WAY 74   EDIT, EDIT, EDIT

In addition to being sensitive to the human implications of your written work, consider the technical aspects, too. Edit your work. Rough drafts are just that – rough. They are the thoughts that you have rapidly put down on paper. Think of your writing as raw data. Like raw data, to make it useful, you have to make something out of it, you have to analyse it. In this instance, editing is analysing. Editing is refining your work to ensure that your message is clear. When you edit:

Check for inconsistencies. Be sure that what you say on page 1 of a report is consistent with what you say on page 49. Be sure that the precise language of a problem statement or research questions remains unchanged as the pages increase.

Link ideas. To help readers follow your thinking, give signals to them by writing introductory paragraphs and introductory sentences. An introductory paragraph states your purpose and describes what the reader should expect to read and in what order. Each paragraph should follow the previous one logically. When you edit, use words to link paragraphs, such as, 'first', 'second', or 'third', or, 'therefore', or 'as a consequence'. They are links between ideas and make your thoughts easier to follow.

Write with nouns and verbs. Effective business writing is to the point. Dickensian or Joycean sentences are not appropriate in business. Write in sentences that are short and simple. Don't overload them with descriptive words, clauses and phrases. The additional verbiage makes it difficult for the reader to find the noun and the verb and thus to decipher your meaning.

Eliminate qualifiers. Qualifiers are words like: 'rarely', 'sort of', 'kind of', 'rather'. They make your writing vague. Relying on words like 'sort of' suggests that you didn't have time to find the right ones initially. For example, she was 'sort of pretty'. Well, was she pretty, stunning, elegant, cute, sensuous or attractive? Eliminate qualifiers and find the words that say what you mean.

Avoid negative expressions. Remember taking exams with questions which began ' Which one of these is not...?' Those questions usually took longer to answer because you had to be sure that you interpreted them correctly. If you use the positive rather than the negative, it is easier for the reader to decipher your meaning.

Beware of ambiguity. In a draft you need not be concerned with words like its, them, that, their, this and those. But be sure to correct them in your final version. Be sure the reader can determine what those pronouns refer to in your sentence. 'We gave the products to the women. They were excellent.' What was 'excellent'? The 'products' or the 'women'?

Keep it simple. Your writing should be clear and uncluttered. Make lists. Use bullet points. Create headings. Tell the reader that a list will follow. Then provide the list. Eliminate tangential information and unnecessary repetition. Remove material that doesn't support your argument. Use words that are easily understood. A 'house' does not need to be an 'abode' or a 'fire' a 'conflagration' just because you are writing a formal report. Keep your words and sentence structure simple.

Check for spelling, grammatical and arithmetical errors. While our software has checks, don't rely on them to the exclusion of your own editing. Double check 'it's' and 'its'; 'their', 'there' and 'they're'; or 'your' and 'you're'. Be sure that plural nouns have plural verbs. In addition, when you reread, check for clarity and correctness. While finding an error in a table is dreadful, finding it before the work is distributed is much better. Be sure that paragraphs haven't been omitted or sentences misplaced. Check to see that numbers add up, that capital letters are used when appropriate, that abbreviations are correct and that punctuation is accurate.

WAY 75   TITLE WELL

This suggestion may sound silly, but select a good title for your report or your memo. Often titles are too short. Titles are intended to help the reader determine what is inside the document. Suppose you write a report and title it 'Mexico'. With an all-encompassing title like that, readers could reasonably expect to read about: food, resorts, climate, flora, fauna, the peso, the government, history, the effect of hurricanes on the economy or an area or on the country, religion, and so on and on. However, if you are writing about the effects of Hurricane Pauline on the tourism market in Cancun, Mexico in 1998, then title your report just that. You are helping your readers. Do the same with your memos.

Fifteen
Writing Letters, Memos and Minutes

We spend many hours writing letters, memos and minutes. These are short pieces of communication, so brief that we often just jot down information quickly. Be careful. Less formal documents should be written as carefully as your longer more formal work.

WAY 76   USE A FORMAT

Whether you are writing a letter or a memo, decide how you want it to look on the page. Most memos begin with:

To:
From:
Date:
Subject:

Sometimes the word 'reference' is used instead of 'subject'. Headings enable the reader to know immediately who sent the memo and what it is about. The date provides you with a record and enables you to track a conversation or discussion of an issue. You can see the sequence of decision-making. Because the memo format is familiar to most people, there is no need to write 'Memo' at the top of the page. Initials next to your name are sufficient rather than a signature.

Letters have a format, too. If you have company letterhead then you don't have to include your address. If you don't use a letter-head, then write your address on the upper right corner of the page. Below, on the left side, write the address of the person to whom the letter is being sent:

Mr John Jones, Secretary
Whatsis Ltd
50 High Street
West Billingsford,
London, X1 2YZ

Dear Mr Jones

And so on.

Even though the letter is addressed to Mr Jones, it's remarkable how often people write 'Dear Sir' for the salutation. Instead, write, 'Dear Mr Jones'.

In both the letters and memos there are usually two or three paragraphs following the salutation. The first paragraph introduces the subject. The middle one or two develop the ideas and the final one states the conclusion, restates your point or calls for action. Letters typically close with 'Yours sincerely' or 'Sincerely yours' followed by your name. Unlike memos, letters are signed.

There are endless variations on memos and letters in terms of style and placement, so consider the use of a 'house style' which we referred to earlier. Having a consistent format projects a professional image for you, your office and your company. It suggests an attention to detail which your audience will appreciate.

WAY 77 RELATE BAD NEWS SENSITIVELY

While image matters, communicating is ultimately about the message, the content. Frequently our messages are not happy ones. Therefore, if you are conveying negative information, such as about plant closures, lay-offs, or denials of requests, put yourself in the other person's shoes. Imagine how you would receive the message if it were written to you. The usual pattern in relaying bad news is to say something positive first, then relate the negative information. That pattern takes some of the sting out of the bad news. The closing sentence speaks of the long-term relationship.

Bad news is bad news and shouldn't be glossed over, but it should be handled with sensitivity.

WAY 78   HANDLE COMPLAINTS CAREFULLY

It is easy to be angered by customers, clients or colleagues when they complain about something you have done. You may feel resentful or unappreciated. You may feel that they haven't understood your position and don't appreciate the situation. Hard as it is, try to view the complaint positively. Realize that the individual has taken the time or had the courage to come forward and express a concern or disappointment about a person, a product, a procedure or a policy. Applaud the fact that you have created a culture which supports openness.

Unfortunately most of us complain to each other rather than to the party who can do something about it. So, when a colleague or client comes forward to express an opinion, you have the opportunity to learn about a problem that may need remedying or that reveals a level of discontent or disappointment. Thank the individual for bringing the matter to your attention, reflect on it, then indicate what steps you intend to take. Avoid false hope or promises that you cannot keep. Again, if you say that you are going to look into the matter or that you are going to remedy it, keep your word.

WAY 79   RECORD DECISIONS

In Way 61 we talked of the importance of keeping minutes and how they allow you to keep track of what has occurred at meetings. Because our days are filled with myriad interactions, it is easy to forget who promised to do what or was asked to follow through on a task. As we saw earlier, keeping track of decisions made at meetings is essential.

When you write your minutes, there is no need to write up the entire discussion that surrounded an issue. While you may have jotted some notes, your written minutes should simply be a record of the decisions and of the actions that were taken. While there may have been a lengthy discussion about the formation of a committee or of the delegation of an assignment, your minutes should indicate what happened. John will set up a committee and report back at the June meeting, By the way, John and you both know one agenda item for your June meeting.

Sixteen
Writing Reports

Reports can be overwhelming for you to write and for your audience to read. Writing reports involves thinking and planning. Well- organized, clearly written reports are helpful for the readers. We write all kinds of reports: accident reports, feasibility studies, progress reports, status reports. There can be written weekly, monthly or annual reports. No matter what the type, let's consider four ways to improve them.

WAY 80   HAVE A STRUCTURE

What follows is the classic structure for a long written report:

- *The title page.* This includes the name of the report, the author and the date.
- *The table of contents.* This is a listing of the sections and page numbers.
- *The introduction.* This includes the terms of reference, a description of the method used in assembling the data and the scope or limitations of the document.
- *The findings.* This includes the facts. It consists of the raw data essential to the study including statistical data, answers to questions, detailed descriptions, numbers, or quotations from interviews.
- *The conclusions.* These are your interpretations of the data analysed in the findings section. The conclusions are consistent with the purpose of your report. Suppose you undertook a study on the use of the company restaurant. One item of your raw data shows that 25 per cent of the staff buy sandwiches in the restaurant, 30 per cent buy coffee and scones. A conclusion might be that more coffee is purchased than sandwiches.

- *The recommendations.* These are suggestions based on your conclusions.
- *The appendixes.* These are the sections at the end of the report that includes letters, diagrams, tables and other raw data. Putting such material in one section at the end rather than throughout the document is less disruptive to your readers.

Not all reports have all these sections, but this is the order in which reports are structured.

WAY 81   CREATE SUB-DIVISIONS

Developing an outline helps you see natural divisions in your material. Suppose you have three sections in your report: introduction, findings and conclusions. As you analyseanalyze your data, however, you realize that your findings section can be broken into different categories. Suppose you interviewed people who eat in the company restaurant for breakfast, for lunch, and for coffee breaks. You might decide that you can make sub-divisions around the three meals, the time of the day or the nature of the purchases. Thus you might divide the findings section into three parts: section A, section B and Ssection C. As a report becomes more complex it begins to look like this:

II Findings

A Breakfast

1 Beverages

a

b

B Lunch

C Coffee Breaks

III Conclusions

Some people prefer a numbering system – 1, 2, 3 with 1.1, 2.1 and 3.1 as subheads and 11.II11 and 2.IIii11 being further sub-divisions.

The structure helpaids you in organizing your material and aids your reader in accessing it.

WAY 82   SEPARATE FACT FROM OPINION

Unless you have been asked for them, keep your opinions out of your reports. Opinions typically appear in the recommendations section of a report only. They are not unsubstantiated views but are supported by data.

Suppose you are writing an accident report involving an employee nameds Sally. In your heart you suspect that Sally caused the accident because of her own carelessness. Unless you can substantiate your views, however, you cannot say so. Be sure that your report records only what happened on the day of the accident. As you assemble the data, you may learn from an unimpeachable source that Sally is a frequent victim of accidents. Having that information may prompt you to create a subsequent report in which you list the dates of previous accidents as well as the nature of those accidents. If you also discover that Sally is the only one who has ever been involved in such accidents, you can conclude that no one else has had any accidents. Therefore, you might recommend that she be given additional training to avoid the problem or that she be transferred to a department where she is not likely to suffer accidents. You cannot do that in your initial accident report if your purpose is to record only what happened. Unless you have the data you cannot characterize Sally as sloppy or lazy. Support your recommendations with facts not assumptions and be wary of generalizing beyond the scope of your data. If you studied only Sally's accident, you cannot discuss others.

WAY 83   DIFFERENTIATE BETWEEN CONCLUSIONS AND RECOMMENDATIONS

Be sure that you don't confuse conclusions with recommendations. Let's consider, a colleague, Mary. She says that she feels warm, has a headache and feels faint. What can you conclude?

Based on the facts, you can conclude that she is unwell – not much more. You do not have enough information to conclude that she has the plague, pneumonia, influenza or is pregnant. Having concluded that she is unwell, you can now recommend a course of action for her. You might suggest that she lie down, go to the nurse or the doctor or take an aspirin, but you cannot do much more. You do not have enough data to suggest that she be hospitalized or quarantined.

In other words, when you make your recommendations about business decisions be sure that your are making basing them on facts not on suppositions.

Seventeen
Using Visuals

We have been focusing on written reports. Now let's look at visuals. They frequently appear in reports or in presentations. Too often, they are hastily put together or expected to reduce a study to one page. Neither situation is ideal. Effective communicators have useful visuals.

WAY 84   UNDERSTAND THEIR PURPOSE

Before preparing visuals, ask yourself why you are using them. If you are designing them because you think that they are nice to have or because everyone seems to use them, then don't use them. If you are using visuals as prompts for you, then don't use them. However, if you believe that visuals clarify or reinforce your message, then by all means include them. Remember visuals are for the audience, not for you. Your objective is to communicate your ideas to the audience. Graphs, charts, artwork, slides and, images are all aids designed to aid the audience's understanding. Visuals aren't supposed to confuse them. Therefore, like all your other communications, design your visuals with the audience in mind.

WAY 85   PREPARE YOUR VISUALS

Your artwork is intended to support your message, so it is essential that your audience can interpret your work. Can they see it? Can they decipher it? Can they relate the images to your words? Suppose your visual is a blueprint or x-ray; are you sure that everyone seeing them knows how to read them?

Now that many of us have access to the internet, we have the opportunity to compare web sites. You know immediately which ones are user friendly and which ones are not. Some are clear, simple and easy to access, others have faint or bold print with indecipherable pictures and cluttered images. What you prefer on a web site should remind you of what works on overheads or slides.

Consider colour combinations. While blue on green may look pretty, black on white is still easier to read. While block lettering may look imposing, the combination of letters in upper and lower case is still easier to decipher. Be sure when you prepare your visual that it clearly depicts what you intended.

WAY 86   TITLE YOUR WORK

Graphs and charts need titles. The audience needs to be told what they are reading or seeing. As we have said we cannot concentrate indefinitely on what we are reading or hearing, our minds work too quickly. We have too many issues to think about. So think of titles as reminders or signposts. Remember also that interruptions occur. People arrive late to meetings or may be called away from them. Reports are not always read in one sitting.

In a presentation, if you are using multiple images, putting a title above or below each image helps the audience stay focused. They are reminded of the relationship of the slide to the points you are making. In written reports, if you are incorporating graphs or tables, be sure to label them as well.

WAY 87   AVOID CLUTTER

Simple is better. Think again about web sites that you have seen. Some are cluttered with links, narrative and advertising. They can be off-putting. If there is too much to see on a page our eyes wander and we wonder where to start reading. It is easier for the reader to follow the flow of the narrative if you keep your images simple. If you want people to recall an image, be sure that your visuals are not buried in too much copy, too many lines or too many numbers. Financial reports in particular are not easy to present visually. Pie charts and bar graphs help. Give some consideration to dividing the data into multiple visuals rather than trying to develop one all-encompassing chart.

When you give a talk, if you have too much information on a given transparency, the audience reads ahead. For example, suppose you have four points on one transparency, they will read points three and four while you still may be discussing point one. It is essential to avoid clutter.

WAY 88   INTRODUCE VISUALS

Advise your audience to expect an upcoming visual. In a written report you signal it by writing something like: 'Graph 102 on page 6 indicates that the gross national product....' In other words, direct your readers' attention to the information. Then help them through it. When you use visuals in a talk, you might direct them by saying, 'Notice the blue bar on the upper left....' Be sure that the audience knows where they are in relationship to what they are seeing. Tourist maps in large cities help readers by marking the spot with the words 'You are here.' These words put the audience in the picture, thus allowing them to interpret the image better. In the case of the tourist map, they now know to turn left or right to find Buckingham Palace. In the same way, it is helpful to signpost in a report.

WAY 89   SAY WHAT YOU SEE

Suppose your slide, transparency or graphic says, 'Mission Statement'. If it does, then say 'Mission Statement' to the audience. Don't say 'Statement of the Mission'. Say aloud the same words you've used in your graphic. Your purpose is to be clear, not to demonstrate to the audience that you have a large vocabulary. You are here to inform, not to be creative about synonyms or phrasing. You want the audience to remember your point.

We retain more when we see and hear the same phrase at the same time. When you say word for word what the audience is seeing in print, you increase the chances of their remembering. Repetition drives your point home. If your image is a list of bullet points, then say each one exactly as it is written.

WAY 90   MORE PRACTICE

Remember to practise with your visuals and your equipment, if you are going to give a talk. Technology has a way of creating unwanted surprises for us:

- Test the computer.
- Know the location of the on/off or power switches.
- Know how to lower and raise a screen.
- Put your flip chart in the best location for your right or left handedness.
- Put your transparencies in order so that you are not thumbing through them for the one that you want.
- Do a run-through with your slides to be sure they are in order.
- Know how to press the advance button on a projector.
- Arrange to be shown how to use an unfamiliar camcorder, VCR or monitor.
- Notice where lights reflect.
- Be sure that you have an extension cable if you need it.
- Be sure that the images you are projecting are dark enough.
- Check sight lines.

The more you practise with your visuals the more you know what angles prevent eye contact, how the microphone feels, what feedback may occur or what echoes are in the room. Decide how and when to distribute handouts. Think about whether the audience will be reading while you are speaking.

By practising you should also be ready with back-up in the event of problems. Know your materials and know your equipment. The only way to do that is to find the time to practice.

Eighteen
Interviewing

In addition to communicating over the phone or with reports and memos, much of what we do in business takes place in face-to-face interviews. We attend interviews and we conduct them. Let's look at ways to improve the interview that you are giving and then look at some ways to improve your performance when you're being interviewed. Although we are talking here primarily about job interviews, the recommendations would be the same for counselling interviews as well.

WAY 91   SELL YOUR ORGANIZATION

When we conduct a job interview, many of us focus on the candidate, on the questions and on the answers being given. Don't forget that throughout the process you are also selling your organization. What precedes the actual interview and what follows it matters. The attitude and behaviour of the people in your organization play a role in the long term relationship with the candidates – whether those candidates are hired or not.

Even if candidates are rejected for positions, they should be made to feel good about their interview experience. Well-written job announcements and letters, timely acknowledgements and polite phone calls all make the organization look good. When candidates are given enough time to schedule interviews, when they receive pertinent correspondence and when they are greeted warmly on the days of interviews, the company appears professional. Interviewers should be on time and be prepared with questions.

Ask yourself: would the applicants say that correspondence was well-written and sent in a timely fashion? That all phone calls were polite? That the interview began on time? That the questioning was gracious, no matter how probing? Even if you did not hire the candidates, will they still feel good about the experience?

Speaking of candidates, unless it is impossible, interview internal candidates. If you do not, you can affect morale and loyalty. Treat people fairly and with dignity. They won't forget. When you treat people unfairly and without dignity, they remember.

WAY 92   LET THE CANDIDATE TALK

One of the most common errors on the part of interviewers is to talk too much. The candidates should talk. What is your objective in the interview process? You want to know as much as possible about the candidates to determine if they will fit into your organization. Even with the inclusion of more and more assessment testing, interviewing is not a scientific process. A wrong hiring decision can be costly. Unfortunately many of those decisions usually have to be made quickly.

The more you know about the candidates the better. The more talking they do, the more that you will learn about them. Therefore, unless you can schedule multiple interviews for each candidate,

- don't spend excessive time describing the organization and yourself;
- avoid asking questions that can be answered with only 'yes' or 'no';
- Ask open-ended questions that require the candidate to talk;
- listen to what they have to say;
- ask follow-up questions like 'why' and 'how' to elicit more information, when they finish their answers.

Sometimes, you can play devil's advocate to determine if they can defend their positions when challenged. Hold reports of your adventures in abeyance. Remember that your goal is to get them to talk.

WAY 93   PREPARE QUESTIONS

Prepare questions that require you to think about the nature of the position you want to fill and the kind of person you need to handle the responsibilities of the job. If you are a member of a panel, work with your colleagues to determine who will ask which questions. You will probably have general questions about the candidates' strengths and weaknesses and others which ask why they left their previous positions. In addition, develop questions that elicit information specific to your organization and to the position.

- Suppose the position requires someone who can work well under pressure. Ask the candidates to describe situations in which they worked under pressure.
- Suppose the job requires knowledge of a subject. Formulate questions which will elicit what they know.
- Suppose the position requires a particular ability. Create fictional situations involving dilemmas, arguments or misunderstandings. Ask the candidates how they might resolve them.

These kinds of questions take time to develop. Prepare them in advance rather than attempting to create them 'off the cuff'. You will have ample opportunity to be spontaneous as you react to the candidates' answers.

WAY 94 DO YOUR HOMEWORK

Now let's reverse roles: you are a candidate and are being interviewed for a position. Suppose you really want to work with Company X. Do your homework.

- Go to the library to read annual reports and business journals.
- Check the company's web site.
- Request copies of current corporate literature, if the company hasn't sent them to you.
- Read the newspaper to see what is happening with Company X and with other organizations in the same industry sector.
- Listen to the news.
- Learn about changing markets.
- Find people who know the company – people who are doing business with the organization. Talk to them. Ask questions about their experiences.

Doing your homework means learning about the industry and about the changes in the company. Knowing that they have been undergoing a major organizational change and have recently launched a new product, or are closing some of their branches will enable you to answer their questions and to ask your own. Your research may whet or dampen your desire to work for them. At the interview, if you are knowledgeable about the organization, you will also be communicating that you want to be perceived as a serious candidate.

WAY 95   PREPARE ANSWERS

Many different interviews include similar questions. In one way or another you will be asked to describe your strengths and weaknesses. You might be asked to identify them or to indicate what you are proudest of, or what you would change about yourself. Sometimes you may be asked why you think that you should be hired or to describe the qualities you would bring to the position. Questions like these should come as no surprise. Therefore, when you prepare for the interview, think how you are going to respond to them. And have answers.

If you submitted a CV, covering letter or application form, keep copies and reread them before you go to the interview. Also reread any job announcements or advertisements to recall exactly the language that is used to describe the position. You will probably be able to anticipate some of the questions. Suppose the company is looking for someone who is detail-oriented. Be ready with examples from your past.

It is unusual for interviews to end without the candidates' being given the opportunity to ask questions. Some may arise naturally in the course of the interview. Something may have been said about building a department or about other changes in the company, and you want to know more. You may want to ask why the position is open, to whom the position reports or what training is provided. Arrive at the interview prepared with questions about the position and about the company, not about salary and benefits.

When you are sure that you will fit into the culture then you should discuss money and benefits. Initially you are interviewing the company to determine if you can and want to work with them.

At the same time, they are determining if you can do the job and fit into their culture.

WAY 96 HAVE EXAMPLES

Suppose you have told the interviewers that you are 'bright, energetic and good with people.' Be ready with evidence to prove it. Think about what you have done in the past and come armed with examples to demonstrate that you are as you describe yourself. Recall situations from your life experience that illustrate those qualities. Refer to those experiences in the context of your application. 'When I was a shop assistant over the Christmas holiday, I had to deal with... '. 'As assistant manager, I frequently... '. Use past experiences to demonstrate your strong qualities. If you are changing fields, show how your abilities and skills transfer to the new position. Being able to motivate people on an athletic team should translate into being able to motivate others in an office.

Nineteen
Putting it All Together

We have separated communication into two parts: communication in general and types of communication. We have looked at theory as well as specific techniques. Now it is time to put communication back together again, to look at it as a whole process.

WAY 97   WATCH OTHER SPEAKERS

One of the best ways to develop as a speaker is to watch other speakers make presentations. Television provides endless opportunities to see news readers, presenters, or politicians in action. At work be particularly attentive to speakers at meetings. As you listen to the content, notice how they structure and sequence their thoughts, how they use examples and analogies. Pay attention to how they present themselves. Look around the room and watch the audience. Notice their reactions. See if the speakers pay attention to the audience's reactions or if they are oblivious to them. Which speakers command attention? Why? Which ones lose the audience? What distracted them? How did a speaker keep the audience engrossed? Was it the delivery? Was it the content? Was it the words, the repetition, the humour? In other words, develop a critical eye. Watch for eye contact and body language. Listen for speech patterns, the use of humour or anecdotes. True, a small meeting is different from a state of the union address, but notice techniques. Watch faces, hands and feet. Notice posture, timing and voice intonation. Evaluate visuals. If an approach or strategy appeals to you, try it. Remember, 'imitation is the sincerest form of flattery'.

But also remember that not everyone else's strategy will work for you. Because we all have different personalities, what is effective for someone else may not be right for you. While some people are comfortable throwing balls in the air or doing somersaults in the conference room, others would be uncomfortable. Don't feel badly. It's just not you. Every time you watch someone, come away with one idea about an approach that you might use or notice a technique that you would want to avoid. Next time perhaps you will smile a bit more or check your watch. Experiment.

WAY 98   READ CAREFULLY

One of the best ways to improve your writing is to read critically. Pay attention to the author's techniques. Are you interested in what is being said? Are you losing interest? Ask yourself why. Ask yourself why a particular report or memo causes you to lose your place or requires you to reread paragraphs. Reflect on why one report is easier to read than another. You may assume that in one instance you were tired. But fatigue may not be the issue at all. Maybe you had difficulty making sense of the author's convoluted sentence structure. Maybe the author didn't define technical terms. Maybe the author made assumptions about what you knew about the background of the situation. Maybe there was no introduction or structure. Notice, too, what is visually attractive about a report and what is not user friendly. Make mental notes and incorporate effective approaches into your own written work.

WAY 99   DEVELOP CRITICAL SKILLS

Feedback keeps you informed about your skills and your development as a communicator. As we said, if people don't volunteer information, then ask. Remember, don't settle for responses like: 'great' 'well done' or 'marvellous'. While those are flattering words to hear, they are not adequate for your needs. You want to know exactly what you did that worked and what you did that didn't work. You may have to ask,

> 'What did you think of the slides?'
> 'How do you feel that I handled the questioning or the question about...?'
> 'What did you think about the layout of the report or the last memo that I sent?'

Train people to give you honest answers. Let them know what you expect from them because you want to replicate what you are doing well or to modify what needs enhancing. You want to apply new ideas. You want to learn from your mistakes and to repeat what works. In other words, you are developing a critical eye and ear.

WAY 100   NETWORK

Read. Share books and videos. Take courses. Find other people with similar interests in communicating well. Create a network of people in other departments who are also eager to develop their talents. If you are anxious about a particular talk or uncomfortable with an aspect of your communication, turn to a colleague. Ask for input or for a quick review. If you do, try not to be defensive about what you are hearing. If you trust your colleagues, understand that they want to help. They may ask you for your help as well. Speaking and writing can make us feel vulnerable. Few of us are comfortable being so exposed. Networking eases the loneliness. Build a network or support system to help you try out ideas or communication strategies.

WAY 101   SEEK OPPORTUNITIES

Speaking in public is frightening. Writing words that become public is daunting. To gain confidence, rather than avoiding the situations, take the opportunities. Do it! It is easier to let someone else give the talk, to never volunteer, to find excuses for not being the one to undertake an uncomfortable situation. The more reports you have to write, the more talks you have to give, the more interviews you have to structure, the better you will become at communicating.

You will learn about your strengths and weaknesses as a communicator. Build on your strengths and diminish your weaknesses. Having done that, you will be better able to share your ideas and feelings with other people. Because you communicate with confidence, you will be more influential and more professional.